TEQUILA

TEQUILA

MYTH, MAGIC & SPIRITED RECIPES

KARL PETZKE

CHRONICLE BOOKS

SAN FRANCISCO

Library of Congress Cataloging-
in-Publication Data available.

ISBN: 978-0-8118-6504-3

Manufactured in China

Design by Myint Design

Pátzcuaro Hot Chocolate recipe, page 122
by Suzanne Tracht. Copyright © 2007 by
Suzanne Tracht. All rights reserved.

Chronicle Books LLC
680 Second Street
San Francisco, California 94107
www.chroniclebooks.com

Campari is a registered trademark of Davide Campari
Milano S.P.A. Cointreau is a registered trademark of
Cointreau Corp. Grand Marnier is a registered trademark
of Societe des Produits Marnier-Lapostolle. Gran Torres
Orange Liqueur is a registered trademark of Torres, Inc.
Midori is a registered trademark of Suntory Limited.
Tabasco is a registered trademark of McIlhenny Co.

ACKNOWLEDGMENTS

A book becomes more than the sum of its parts on completion. It takes on its own life, becoming larger than the individual efforts it took to produce it. *Tequila* has been no different. When I first proposed this book, I had a pretty good idea of the people I wanted to collaborate with. Some were collaborators from before, and some were new and untested in a book project such as this one. For all of his knowledge and passion for tequila, Julio Bermejo has been instrumental in my research and understanding of tequila, its origins, and its process. To his wife, Lily, and her family in Arandas, Mexico, thank you for opening the doors of your distillery and embracing this project. To my writer, Carolyn Miller, thank you again for approaching *Tequila* with same enthusiasm I have for it. Your words became the voice and underlying spirit of this book. Food stylists Dan Becker and Jen Straus created classic and innovative recipes using tequila as an ingredient—thank you both for these amazing recipes and beautiful food styling. Thank you Suzanne Tracht for your Pátzcuaro hot chocolate recipe, soon to be everyone's favorite. To my editors and constant sources of support at Chronicle Books, Bill LeBlond, Amy Treadwell, and Sarah Billingsley, as well as Vanessa Dina, Jane Chinn, and Doug Ogan, thank you for your patience throughout this project. To my friends Elisa Eurbanelli and Celeste McMillin thank you for your editing and printing expertise. To the producers I met in Mexico, especially Jaime Giovannini and Guillermo Sauza: Without your generous insight and amazing tequila, this book would not be complete. And to my book designer, Karin Myint, thank you for putting the beauty of your vision in this book. You created a visually stunning story from a palette of words, photography, and cuisine. Thank you all. —Karl Petzke

FOR YOUR LOVE, TO KARIN AND UMA RIE

CONTENTS

9   The Road to Tequila

15   Heart: Earth and Agave

23   Myth: Origins and Mystique

32   Time Line

35   Pride: Tequila Culture

49   Soul: Essence of the Fermented Nectar

60   Bebidas ∾ Tequila Cocktails

84   Cocina Salada ∾ Savory Tequila-Inspired Dishes

110   Cocina Dulce ∾ Tequila and Agave Desserts

124   A Tequila Glossary

126   Index

128   Table of Equivalents

Traveling in Mexico while photographing this book, I caught a lift from Guadalajara to Tequila with a man named Tomas, a friend of a contact in Guadalajara. We went the back way to Tequila, staying off the main highways and following the two-lane roads between towns. It was getting late, and we decided to stop for food at a roadside stand, where we ate carnitas tacos and drank shots of tequila made by the man who owned the stand. He showed us his slightly misshapen handmade copper still, which couldn't have held more than about five liters, and I learned that it was not unusual for such small proprietors to make their own tequila. The tacos were excellent, and so was the tequila, which we drank from the narrow shot glasses called *caballitos.* We started out with *blanco,* then moved on to some surprisingly good *reposado.*

I woke up on the bench seat of Tomas's pickup truck, keys in the ignition, sun in my face. Tomas had vanished. There was no one around, nobody at all. The roadside stand was nowhere to be seen, and the landscape was completely different from last evening. No mountains on the horizon, just hills like swells on the ocean, and scrub trees as far as I could see. I wasn't sure how I got there, or where *there* was.

I tried to start the pickup. The engine turned over, but it wouldn't start. I was either out of gas or had an unknown mechanical problem. The gas gauge showed empty, but how would I know it actually worked? In the bed of the truck were two cases of tequila that must have been from last night's roadside proprietor. I opened one, hair of the dog. I stuffed the bottle in my camera bag. I decided to leave the rest, but not before giving a proper burial in a rock outcropping one hundred steps off the road. Someday I will be back. I drew a map of landmarks. I left the keys to the truck in the ignition. I started walking.

THE ROAD TO TEQUILA

THE ROAD TO TEQUILA

Mexico with its prickly pear and its serpent; Mexico blossoming and thorny, dry and lashed by hurricane winds, violent in outline and color, violent in eruption and creation, surrounded me with its magic and its extraordinary light.

—Pablo Neruda, *Memoirs*

HEART

HEART

EARTH AND AGAVE

In the high plains and valleys of Jalisco, row upon row of agave plants erupt from the soil like stiff, blue-gray fountains. Each swordlike leaf of this native succulent is lightly scalloped on the edges with small, curving, light red thorns, and ends in an erect, sharp spike. But hidden in the core of every armored plant is its heart, growing sweeter and sweeter with each passing day until the agave is ready to send up its flowering shoot. That is when the crown of leaves is cut away to reveal the heart, heavy with the sap that will be transformed into the clear liquor of tequila.

Sweet and bitter, blossoming and thorny, a succulent that grows in semiarid soil, the blue agave plant embodies Mexico in all its contradictions and complexity. Though other species of agave grow as far north as the southwestern United States, and many different kinds are found throughout Mexico, especially in the central highlands, the blue agave grows only in the high valleys and uplands of Jalisco, parts of its bordering states, and in the state of Tamaulipas. Made in the heart of the country from the heart of an indigenous plant, by a technique imported by the Spanish invaders, who learned it from the Moorish invaders of Spain, tequila—cold and fiery, breathtaking and sustaining—is emblematic of Mexico.

HEART

HEART

The Mesoamericans had many gods, and their gods gave them many gifts: corn, tobacco, cocoa, agave. The most demanding god was the sun, who required human blood to keep rising every day, but the sun was also the most essential of gods, for only the light of the sun made possible the gifts of the earth. These sacred plants sprang from the soil, and could be cultivated and harvested to yield magical substances. But none of them had as many beneficial uses as the agave, including the ability of pulque, its fermented nectar, to make its imbibers brave and joyous.

Like any food product, tequila, the distilled juice of the agave, is the result of a linked group of factors: the type of soil, the elevation of the agave field above sea level, the range and duration of temperature and the amount of rain during the growing season, the care in cultivation and harvesting, and the level of ripeness of the blue agave at harvest. Only the care in cultivation and harvesting is under the control of the agave farmer; the rest is up to chance or, as the Mesoamericans believed, the gods. There is no way of knowing exactly when an agave will ripen: even in a field of agaves all planted at the same time, one plant can ripen years ahead of another. Experience and careful attention are required to judge ripeness: typically, the plant appears to be shrinking slightly when it reaches the stage of sending up its flower spike.

Tequila is the ultimate product of a unique plant grown in a unique place; it is quintessentially Mexican. Encapsulated in its unique taste is the wonder the ancient inhabitants of that land must have felt when they first understood that the strange, spiky plants carpeting their high deserts were the source of a life-giving liquid unlike any other.

- Agave sap can be converted into agave nectar, crystallized into a sugar, fermented into pulque, and distilled into mezcal or tequila.

- The Aztecs used agave leaves as roof tiles and the stalks as beams. Fiber from the leaves was used to make paper, rope, thread, mats, and cloth.

- Agave leaves are used to line barbecue pits.

- The skin of the leaves can be stripped off and used to wrap a dish of barbecued lamb called *mixtote*.

- The worms that feed on the agave plant are sometimes added to bottles of mezcal; they are actually the caterpillars of moths, and are also fried and eaten, while the eggs of ants that live under agave plants are cooked into a stew called *escalmol*. Some bottles of mezcal have small packets of a dark red powder attached to them; this is a mixture of ground dried agave worms, dried chiles, and salt, which is also commonly served in small bowls in Oaxacan restaurants as a condiment to sprinkle over food.

- The agave heart and the flower shoot can be baked and eaten; the flowers are also edible.

- The hollow dried flower stalk is used as a musical instrument similar to a didgeridoo.

- The discarded leaves of the harvested agave are used for compost in the agave fields.

AGAVE NECTAR

Agave nectar, produced from the heart of the agave plant like mezcal and tequila, has so many beneficial qualities that it has come to be thought of as a kind of gift from the gods. This ancient food was produced in Mexico long before the arrival of the Spanish, but it has been discovered anew in the United States recently, especially among vegans and lovers of natural foods. Like honey, it is a natural sweetener, but it is not an animal product. And unlike honey (and cane and beet sugars), it is low on the glycemic index, which means it can be used by diabetics and people on low-carbohydrate diets. Agave nectar is not only sweeter than sugar, it is organic, highly nutritious, and a form of soluble fiber.

The process of making agave nectar begins with the harvesting of the ripe hearts of the agave plant. (Various types of agave are used, including the blue agave; some products are labeled as 100 percent blue agave.) Rather than being cooked completely, as they are in the making of tequila and mezcal, the hearts are heated only to 118°F—the point at which they begin to release their sap. The hearts are then chopped, filtered, and sent through a centrifuge to further separate out solids. The result is a syrup, thinner than honey, that is used to sweeten liquids and in cooking. Agave nectar is available in several grades: light, amber, and dark amber. Some of the recipes in this book are made using agave nectar; it has a natural affinity with tequila, and so is often used in tequila drinks. It also complements tropical and semi-tropical fruits, and is especially compatible with pork and chicken. And combining agave nectar with chiles seems to heighten the flavor of both foods, setting off sparks from the chiles and deepening the sweetness of the agave nectar.

MYTH

MYTH

ORIGINS AND MYSTIQUE

"When it was still night, in the dark, the gods assembled." And they created human-kind. "Let there be light," exclaims the Mayan Bible, the *Popul Vuh*. "Let the dawn rise on heaven and earth. There shall be no glory until the human creature exists."

—Carlos Fuentes, *The Buried Mirror*

The story of tequila begins with the myth-ridden world of the ancient Mesoamericans and their mingled religions of bloodthirsty gods. It continues with the arrival of the Spanish and their general Hernán Cortés, who was first seen as a reborn god, but unleashed carnage on the Aztecs to equal their own on their sacrificial victims. The Spanish brought a new god, and his divine son, and the divine mother, Mary, and so the old gods were replaced, though the memory of them lives on in a shadow world not far removed from this one.

The Aztec empire reached its height at the same time it was destroyed, less than five centuries ago. The Aztec monuments that Cortés destroyed in order to build Mexico City, literally on top of them, are appearing again from beneath the pavement, like the Paricutin volcano that suddenly emerged in a cornfield alongside a Mexican farmer on February 20, 1943.

MYTH

"Every kind of magic is always appearing and reappearing in Mexico," wrote Pablo Neruda, citing the appearance of that 1943 volcano as one instance. But there are many other kinds of magic here, from a culture that was born in blood and subjugation but that has endured against all odds to a country that has developed a complex civilization from such striking contrasts of peoples, beliefs, and traditions.

As Mexican novelist Ilan Stavans writes, "In Mexico, reality and fiction, history and fantasy, braid in a mysterious, labyrinthine way and nothing is simple." Though it is a land with many problems today, it is also a land with many pleasures: the warm beaches of the Pacific and Atlantic coasts; the rich native cultures with their own languages, clothing, foods, and art forms; the deserts and mountains and high plains; the temperate and semitropical forests; the crumbling and burgeoning colonial cities; the archaeological traces of ancient civilizations; the omnipresent past; the acceptance of death and the nearness of the spirit world; the love of the fiesta and the sense of expanded time; the music that is always playing somewhere and the flowers that fill the churches and are bunched in plastic buckets on the street corners; the mark of the human hand in everyday objects like pottery and glass; the love of color; the delight in the whimsical and the devotion to hard work; the sense of life taking place on the streets. The seductions of food and drink are a fine pleasure as well: the full Mexican breakfast, from *bolillos* and jam to black beans and eggs and tortillas, hot chocolate and *churros*; the elemental taste of chiles in rustic sauces dating back to the Mayans; the clarity and clean taste of Mexican beer; the festivals of seafood and fruits in the markets; the aroma of tortillas from street stands and food stalls; and not least of all, the taste of a fine tequila at the end of a long, light-filled day.

PULQUE

Behind every bottle of tequila is the ghost of pulque, the pre-Columbian alcoholic drink that is still popular in Mexico. The earliest depiction of pulque is found in stone carvings dating to A.D. 200, but there is no doubt that it was being produced many centuries earlier, for it is integral to the ancient myths that underlie Mexican culture. Like mezcal, pulque, called *octli poliqhui* or *octli* by the Aztecs, is made from the fermented juice of the agave plant, but it is not distilled, as this technology was unknown in Mexico until the Spanish imported stills in the years following the Conquest.

The production of pulque is simple: When the agave plant is between eight and ten years old, a swelling forms on the top of its central cone, a sign that its flower stalk will soon emerge. The swelling is punctured, which kills the stalk but allows the sweet, milky sap that the plant has produced to feed its flowers to gather in the agave's cone for several months. Eventually, the swelling rots and is dug out, leaving a hole in the top of the cone, which repeatedly fills with agave sap. The milky liquid is removed each day for as long as the plant supplies it—usually about two months. This *aguamiel* ("honey water"), slightly sweet and refreshing, is fermented in large barrels and sold fresh in pulque bars called *pulquerías*. Although fairly low in alcohol—4 to 8 percent—it has a sudden unexpected kick, a somewhat slimy texture, and a unique sour-sweet taste that is an acquired one. Fruit is often mixed in with pulque to make it more palatable.

For both the Mayans and the Aztecs, pulque was regarded as such a potent and magical drink that it was reserved for a select group of citizens. Mayan shamans used it as a means to access the spirit world (along with peyote and marijuana), and Aztec priests used it as an intoxicant in the religious ritual of auto-sacrifice (the terminal thorns of the agave, as well as other sharp objects, were used by the priests in the practice of bloodletting, in which they pierced their own tongue, ear lobes, penis, or buttocks). Both the priests and the victims in the rituals of human sacrifice also imbibed pulque, as did the nobility and warriors in other religious and ceremonial rites. Because pulque is rich in vitamins and nutrients, the Aztecs allowed elderly people (age fifty-two and over) and pregnant and nursing women to drink it. Otherwise, commoners were allowed to drink pulque only during a five-day period at the end of the Aztec calendar year, the Day of the Dead festival. After the destruction of the Aztec empire, pulque became available to anyone who could acquire it, and was a factor in destroying the indigenous population.

Because pulque is drunk fresh (it can spoil in as little as twenty-four hours), it remains a local drink. (Canned preserved pulque does exist, but it is considered an inferior product.)

MYTH

Pulque has many deities, including Tepoztecatl, a lesser god. (He has a town named for him—Tepoztlán—and his own pyramid, where pulque festivals are still held.) Tepoztecatl is said to be accompanied by four hundred even lesser deities, the gods of drunkenness, who take the form of rabbits. The rabbit gods derive from one of the many pulque creation myths: A farmer's wife, named Mayahuel, was chasing rabbits from her agave field when she noticed one rabbit staggering around in a circle. After she learned that it had been drinking fermented agave sap, she and her husband drank some as well and discovered that it caused both happiness and fearlessness.

As often happens to those to whom great secrets are revealed, Mayahuel eventually became a goddess, and is sometimes pictured as springing from an agave. As a goddess, she became an agave, or the agave became her, in the shape-shifting way of the divine. She was said to have four hundred nipples or four hundred breasts, all of which produced pulque, a milky substance that looks like human breast milk, to nourish the four hundred rabbit gods of drunkenness.

The Aztecs honored the four hundred gods by judging the levels of pulque intoxication on a rabbit scale: the lowest state of drunkenness was the domain of the god named One Rabbit, while the highest was that of the god Four Hundred Rabbit, going far beyond the common definition of drunkenness as seeing double. Just as the Greeks and Romans poured a bit of wine on the ground as an offering to the gods, in *pulquerías* some drinkers still spill a little pulque on the floor as a tribute to the god Ometotchli, also known as Two Rabbit.

Even with its growing popularity, tequila keeps dragging modern myths along with it. One of the hoariest misconceptions is that some tequila bottles contain a worm. In reality, only some less-expensive mezcals are bottled with one of the caterpillars that feed on the agave plant. A surprising number of people believe that tequila is made from a cactus. The agave is actually a desert succulent, and a member of the lily family, even though it is thorned like a cactus. Other myths are that tequila and mezcal are the same thing (tequila is a unique kind of mezcal), that tequila is a hallucinogen and that it does not cause hangovers (it is an inebriant, and as with any other liquor, overindulging will indeed cause the drinker to be sorry the next day), that it is a kind of homebrew (Mexico does produce a number of different homebrews made from the agave, but tequila is highly regulated by the government of Mexico), and that all tequilas taste alike (there is a wide variation in taste among tequilas, based on *terroir*—that trendy French term meaning a specific growing region—along with climate, production, and style, among other factors).

TEQUILA VS. MEZCAL

Tequila-lovers have a saying: All tequilas are mezcals, but not all mezcals are tequilas. Both mezcal and tequila are made from the agave plant, and for both liquors the plant is ripened and harvested in the same way: The plant's flower stalk is cut off just as it begins to grow. The core of the plant, now being fed with the nutrients that would have produced the flower stalk, swells into a huge juicy heart, which is harvested by cutting off the plant's stiff, thorny leaves. For both mezcal and tequila, the massive heart, or *piña,* which can weigh from 80 to 150 pounds, is cooked to convert all its starches into sugars, then crushed to drain off the juice, which is then fermented and distilled.

The tendency these days, however, since tequila has become so popular and so high in quality, is to put it in a category of its own. A good argument can be made for this separation, as tequila is produced by a different process than mezcal, which is roasted over rocks heated with wood charcoal in underground pits, giving it its characteristic smoky flavor. Tequila, by contrast, is cooked by steam in above-ground brick-and-stone ovens or autoclaves. Originally, mezcal was distilled only once, but today it is distilled twice, as are the better tequilas. Though fermented in wooden vats, mezcal today is aged in stainless-steel tanks; *reposado* and *añejo* tequilas are aged in oak barrels, which gives them a woody taste. Unlike mezcal, tequila is also denomination controlled, which means that any liquor with that name must be produced not just in Mexico but in a specific region of that country, centered around the town of Tequila in the state of Jalisco and in some small areas of other states. It may, however, be bottled outside of Mexico, though premium tequilas are bottled only in that country.

But the most important distinction is that tequila must be made from at least 51 percent blue agave, while mezcal is made from one of eight different varieties of agave, not including the blue agave. The blue agave is found only on the high west-central plains in the region of Tequila.

c. 200,000 B.C.

The Volcán de Tequila erupts, spreading ash over a radius of more than one hundred miles. Blue agave plants begin to flourish in the rich volcanic soil.

c. 6000 B.C.

Agriculture begins in Mexico, as some indigenous peoples start to cultivate corn using selective breeding. The agave is cultivated for food, and its fiber is used to make rope and cloth. The sap of the agave, a highly nutritious liquid and natural sweetener, is almost certainly being collected, and accidental fermentation undoubtedly takes place at some point, yielding pulque. (Fermentation can take place naturally in the plant itself once the flower stalk has been removed.)

c. 1600 B.C.

Corn begins to be intensively farmed, and several native groups develop advanced cultures over the next fifteen hundred years. Undoubtedly pulque is deliberately produced, and creation myths are developed to explain its origin.

A.D. 250 to 650

Mayan civilization flourishes. Pulque is one of the mind-altering substances used by shamans to access visions.

1521 through 1535

The Spanish continue to explore Mexico, including the area that is today Jalisco. The first Spanish monks arrive in 1523. Mexico becomes New Spain in 1535. Mexico City begins to rise on the ruins of Tenochtitlán. All restrictions on the drinking of pulque are ended. The Spanish bring still pots to Mexico and begin production of mezcal from the juice of the maguey plant.

1753

Maguey plants are given the generic Greek name agave by Swedish botanist Carl Linnaeus.

1758

The first mezcal distillery is legally registered by José Antonio Montaño Cuervo in the town of Tequila.

1873

Don Cenobio Sauza begins to use only blue agave in the production of his mezcal, and other producers follow suit. The name "tequila" is officially adopted for mezcal from the Tequila region. Tequila is legally exported to the United State for the first time.

1902

The blue agave variety is named Agave azul tequilana Weber, after botanist Franz Weber.

A.D. 1325

The Aztecs, who have entered the high central plateau from the north, found their capital city, Tenochtitlán. Their religion incorporates earlier elements from the Olmecs and Mayans; the agave is considered sacred, and pulque is an integral part of religious rituals and is reserved for the nobility, warriors, and priests.

February, 1519

Hernán Cortés and his army land in Veracruz. In his first letter to King Carlos V, he writes: "They sell honey emanated from corn that is as sweet as the sugar obtained from a plant they call maguey and from these plants they make wine and sugar, which they sell."

November, 1519

Cortés and his men enter Tenochtitlán and are welcomed by Moctezuma, the Aztec emperor. The Spanish observe the Aztec drinking pulque.

August, 1521

Cuauhtémoc (the ruler of Tenochtitlán after the death of Moctezuma) is captured, and the Aztec Empire ends.

1930

An increased demand for tequila, combined with a limited supply, causes producers to develop *mixto* tequilas, which are only 51 percent blue agave.

1941 to 1945

Tequila production booms during World War II as liquor production is halted in the United States and Europe.

1950s and 1960s

American tourists begin to vacation in Mexico and experience the delights of tequila.

1964

José Cuervo gold tequila is imported into the United States and becomes a favorite with the drinking public.

1990s

Bars specializing in a wide variety of tequilas, including premium tequilas, open in various cities in Mexico, and the trend spreads to the United States.

2000s

Premium tequila achieves status as a fine liquor on the level of French Cognac.

PRIDE

PRIDE

TEQUILA CULTURE

Like coffee and love, tequila is irresistible, demanding, and powerful. Like coffee and love, tequila is not for the half-hearted. With all its purity, immediacy, and vertigo . . . it is a drink for the initiated. . . .

—Vicente Quirarte

The town of Tequila is not one of the elegant baroque cities the Spanish constructed across the vast country of Mexico. Though there are a few formal, ornamented stone and stucco structures in the very center of town, most of the architecture belongs to the school of low cement-block buildings with corrugated plastic or tin roofs. Tequila, with a population of about twenty thousand, is situated in a high valley (four thousand feet above sea level) midway between Guadalajara and Puerto Vallarta. The first sign that you're approaching the birthplace of tequila is the giant billboards shaped like tequila bottles appearing surreally against the high-desert sky in the scrubby fields.

The entire town, from its *jimadora* fountain and its statue of Mayahuel, the goddess of agave, to its billboards and distilleries and bars, is devoted to tequila, and the valley is filled with row after row of agaves, stretching off into a blue-gray haze against the horizon. The town, founded by the Spanish in 1530, rests at the foot of Mount Tequila, an extinct volcano.

To the east of the valley, past Guadalajara and centered around the village of Arandas, are the highlands known as Los Altos (in Spanish) or Atotonilco (in Náhuatl), where more agave fields cover the hills.

Although there are a little over one hundred registered producers of tequila, and about forty thousand people who work in the industry, there are only fifty to sixty distilleries. José Cuervo has built a showcase distillery in the town of Tequila itself, but most tequila distilleries, or *fabricantes,* are modest affairs; many are small, nondescript buildings, with little signage or evidence of any activity. An air of secrecy, or mystery, hangs over them, along with the ripe, fruity, and vegetal odor of cooked agave hearts.

The process of making tequila is surprisingly uncomplicated. It is, in essence, the same process that was used by the first Spaniards who imported pot stills from Spain: ripe agave *piñas,* or hearts, are halved or quartered, cooked, crushed, fermented, filtered, and distilled.

Not surprisingly, just as every detail of the growing conditions affects the size and sweetness of each agave heart, every step of the distillation process affects the final tequila. What was once essentially a handmade product is today increasingly industrialized, but, also not surprisingly, every attempt to speed up the ancient process seems to affect the end product in a negative way.

The traditional method of steaming the *piñas* in huge above-ground brick-and-stone ovens distinguishes the production of tequila from that of mezcal, which is cooked in underground pits.

In a step that takes from 36 to 48 hours, the agave hearts cook between 135°F to 145°F to convert their carbohydrates to sugar. As they cook, the hearts turn the dark color of yams, and the air fills with a combined fragrance of molasses and caramel. After cooking, the hearts cool for 24 to 36 hours. The more modern method, however, is to steam the hearts in stainless-steel autoclaves, which are basically giant pressure cookers. The autoclave method uses higher temperatures, which cuts the combined cooking and cooling time to as little as 8 hours, but the higher temperatures also negatively affect the taste of the final liquor.

During the cooking process, any juice that leaks from the hearts is collected, then cut with water, and added to the liquid retrieved from the crushed cooked hearts that is to be fermented. In the traditional method of crushing the hearts, the *piñas* are carried to a shallow stone pit, where they are flattened by a giant circular stone (the *tahona*) attached to the end of a pole anchored in the center of the pit. The stone was originally powered by men and then burros, but today tractors are used. The modern method involves mechanical steel crushers, which the majority of producers use today.

In a traditional step that is still used in a few distilleries, the pulp is transferred to a deeper stone pit where it is mixed by the hands and feet of naked men to further separate the fiber from the pulp and to begin the fermentation process. Supposedly, the wild yeasts found naturally on the human body help to ferment the pulp, which is so high in acid that it can destroy clothing.

The juice (*mosto,* or must) is then transferred to stainless-steel or wooden tanks and mixed with yeast to start the fermentation process. These days, many distilleries use commercial yeasts with accelerants added to cut the fermentation time to one or two days, but the better tequilas are fermented with a natural yeast culture developed and maintained by the distillery, like the years-old proprietary "mother" that traditional bakeries use to leaven sourdough bread. Natural fermentation of the must takes much longer than the short-cut method—from seven to ten days—but again, the traditional method produces a superior tequila. The abbreviated methods are used almost exclusively in the production of less-expensive *mixtos* and gold tequilas.

Next, the fermented must is filtered and, finally, distilled. The original stills the Spanish brought to Mexico were made of clay. Both tequila and mezcal are still distilled in clay stills, with those bottles labeled with the phrase *de olla.* Today, most distilleries use either huge copper pot stills (also called alembic stills) or newer stainless-steel stills called column stills. The science of the still is basic: An alcoholic liquid is heated to its boiling point in the container; the alcohol and water evaporate, but since alcohol evaporates at a lower temperature than water, the vapor is richer in alcohol than water. The vapor flows through a pipe or coil, which cools and condenses it, leaving an alcohol-rich liquid. The process is repeated to yield a liquid that is even higher in alcohol.

The stainless-steel column stills are preferred by makers of *mixto* and gold tequilas, because only one distillation is thought necessary, but the better tequilas continue to be made in copper stills, and are distilled twice.

The clear liquid, now an 80-proof (40 percent alcohol) *blanco* tequila, is either bottled as *blanco* or taken to the *bodega* (aging room), where it is transferred to oak barrels (usually old barrels once used to age whisky, which moderates the oak taste imparted to the tequila) to age into *reposado* or *añejo*. The final step is the blending of the aged tequilas. The blender combines tequilas from different barrels in order to maintain the taste of a specific brand of *resposado* or *añejo* from year to year. The journey of the agave ends with the transportation of each bottle to a bar or liquor store shelf, and the blooming of its liquor in a glass, where the body and aroma of tequila can be savored in all its heady power.

FIVE TEQUILAS

The five kinds of tequilas vary based on their age and contents (gold tequila has additives). They may be made from either 100 percent pure agave tequila or a *mixto* tequila, which is at least 51 percent pure agave mixed with another sugar (or sugars).

Blanco: "White," or silver (*plata,* in Spanish) tequila is the clear liquid resulting from the second and final distillation. *Blanco* is valued for its strong agave flavor, which has been described by some as vegetal, and by one aficionado as having the combined flavors of white pepper and grass. *Blanco* may be either pure 100 percent agave, or a *mixto*.

Oro ("gold"): Called *joven* ("young") and sometimes *abocado* ("semisweet") or *suave* ("smooth"), gold tequila is a *blanco* with caramel or other additives mixed in to give it the recognizable color and sweeter, smoother taste of a *resposado*. All gold tequilas are *mixtos*.

PRIDE

Reposado: "Rested" tequila, the most popular type, is *blanco* that has been aged in wooden barrels for at least two months and up to one year. The barrels, which are made of either oak or holm oak, give the tequila a light golden color, while the aging process smooths the edge of the agave taste and adds the faint oaky taste. *Reposado* is usually 100 percent agave tequila, but can be *mixto* as well.

Añejo: "Aged" tequila is stored for at least one year in wooden barrels, which gives it a stronger oak flavor and a darker color than *reposado.* It is usually, but not always, made with 100 percent agave tequila. The better *añejos* are usually eighteen months to three years old. These tequilas are now confusingly referred to as "extra-aged" rather than just "aged," to distinguish them from *reposados.* They may also be called "vintage."

Extra-añejo: Also called *maduro,* or "extra-aged," as well as "vintage," these tequilas are at least three years old. This new category dates back to 2006, when the industry created it in response to the demands of producers. Because tequila is believed to deteriorate in taste after five years in the barrel, many producers age it for three years in the barrel, then transfer it to stainless-steel tanks for a total aging time of as many as seven and even ten years, yielding expensive bottlings that are said to compare in quality with the finest French Cognacs. Distilleries are also experimenting with different sizes of barrels and different woods to alter the final taste of the aged tequila.

Other tequila terms include *reserva,* or *reserva de casa* or *reserva de familia,* which usually refers to an *añejo* or *reposado* in limited production. *Muy añejo* and *tres añejos* once referred to tequilas aged for more than three years, but these terms are no longer used. *Gran reposado* (aged longer than eleven months) and *blanco suave* (a *blanco* that is smoother than the norm) are currently used in marketing, but they are not official terms.

Ian Chadwick, the guru of tequila, points out that one reason for the current fascination with tequila is the wide variety in taste from one kind of tequila to another. Not only are there the five outlined main categories, but there is variation within the categories depending on the amount of blue agave in the liquor. Chadwick further notes that there are also taste variations based on how the tequila is made, as well as where and how the plants are grown: tequilas from the highlands differ in taste from those made with agaves grown in the valley, for example. All of these variations give tequila the multiplicity of flavors that make it a field of passionate study for lovers of fine spirits.

PREMIUM TEQUILAS

Though there is no legal definition of the term, the words *premium tequila* have allowed the tequila industry to make a quantum leap in just the last few years. To some, the term means tequila made only from 100 percent blue agave. To others, it applies only to *reposado* and *añejo* tequilas. And another definition is tequila that has been made in limited quantities with extraordinary care. In general, it means a high-quality tequila marketed at the level of fine French Cognac and imbibed the same way: slowly savoring every sip, without ice or any added ingredients, as an exquisite after-dinner drink.

Just to complicate the issue, the terms "super-premium" and "ultra-premium" are also used, and there is even an occasional reference to "super ultra-premium tequila." Tequilas with these designations have some claim to quality that goes beyond their pure blue agave content; super-premiums are usually either *reposados* or *añejos,* while ultra-premiums are usually *añejos* that have been distilled more than the usual two times.

Premium tequilas are further distinguished by their cost. They are considerably more expensive than nonpremiums, and as you ascend the premium scale, prices increase from around $30 to a heart-stopping $150. Most of the time, the level of quality is mirrored by the uniqueness of the tequila bottle and the ebullience of the label design. Here is where Mexican ingenuity and creativity take flight: The bottle may be elegantly elongated or shaped like a squat brandy decanter; other forms mimic a tequila aging barrel, a sunburst, a straight bottle inside a circular bottle, and a saddle resting on top of a wooden stump. The caps may be foil-wrapped or topped with round corks that resemble Champagne corks; round decanter-style stoppers are also popular. The glass may be extra thick, fluted, patterned like a *piña,* black or one of various shades of blue, or filled with bubbles or what look like flecks of gold; one tequila is bottled in porcelain with inlays of pewter and blue ceramic. The labels are usually exuberantly florid, illustrated with the figure of a *charro,* a blue agave plant, a *jimador* (the worker who harvests the agave hearts), a Mexican eagle (a symbol found on the Mexican flag and coat of arms), or any combination of the above, along with guns, a rifle, a sombrero, and a wide range of garlands, flourishes, and elaborate typefaces. In fact, the variety of shapes, colors, and designs adds to the desirability of premium tequilas as gift and celebration liquors at the same time as they mirror the Mexican love of the inventive and the baroque.

SOUL

SOUL

ESSENCE OF THE FERMENTED NECTAR

Tequila village sits at the base of a volcanic cinder cone that the locals call Tequila Mountain. The mountain rises about 3,500 feet above the surrounding terrain . . . and dominates the scenic area for miles.

—Bob Emmons, *The Book of Tequila*

The soul of tequila is in the soil of Jalisco. In the valley of Tequila and on the flanks of its extinct volcano, the soil is dark brown, rich with volcanic ash; in the highlands of Los Altos, it is tinted a deep red with iron oxide. In both places, the soil glitters with minerals and bits of crushed obsidian.

And in both places, the blue agave fields stretch out under the sun. Mayahuel, the goddess of the agave, was worshipped as a fertility goddess for good reason: the agave has three ways of propagating itself, tripling its odds for surviving in a hostile semiarid climate. Like the ginger plant, it sends out rhizomes underground; these sprout roots and develop into new agaves. These daughter agaves are harvested by tequila producers and moved to nurseries to continue growing until they are the right size for replanting.

Wild agaves have two more modes of propagation: Between the ages of four and six years, they send up a flower stalk whose blossoms are pollinated by one of several different species of bats that have evolved just to drink their nectar, thereby spreading agave pollen. The fertilized flowers produce berries containing seeds, and in the wild, these are propagated by animals and humans. Once they have flowered and fruited, the agaves die. But during their fertile period, wild agaves have yet another means of continuing their line: asexual flowers, called "leaf axil bulblets," appear on the sides of the flower stalk; these fall to the earth and root themselves to become new agaves. In some agaves, miniature plants that appear on the sides of the mother plant can also be removed and rooted. It's no wonder that the agave, with its milky liquid, its abundance, its fertility, and its capacity for nourishment, was believed to embody the spirit of a female deity.

THE WAYS WE LOVE TEQUILA

Purists insist that the best way to enjoy tequila is to slowly sip a premium *añejo* from a brandy snifter. But the ways to enjoy this potent liquid are myriad. Traditional *charro* style, adopted by Americans visiting Mexico and Mexican bars and restaurants in the United States, is the salt/lime/shot method. In the United States, it's usually done by drinking from a traditional shot glass and licking the salt from the hollow between the thumb and index finger of one hand (after licking the skin first to encourage the salt to adhere), but the authentic method is to drink from a long, narrow two-ounce shot glass called a *caballito*, or "pony." (The *caballito's* shape is derived from the original tequila tasting glass: a bull's horn, cut off at the bottom to form a level surface for resting on a bar.) A small amount of salt is placed on the back of the nondominant hand, which is held taut, with the fingers outstretched. The hand is raised to a few inches from the mouth, and the outstretched fingers are struck with the dominant hand, making the salt leap into the mouth. Next, the drinker sucks on a lime wedge and takes a sip of tequila (not the whole glass). The ritual is repeated five or six times until the *caballito* is empty.

In both Mexican and U.S. drinking rituals, there is, of course, the simple downing of whole shots of tequila—tequila shooters—sans salt or lime in a variety of circumstances, including slamming the bottom of the shot glass on the bar immediately after swallowing the contents. This is often followed by the dimming of vision, altered walking patterns, and unexpected events, like waking up in the morning in a room other than your own.

A popular Mexican drink that has not (yet) hit the United States is the combination of tequila and Coca-Cola, with a pinch of salt, the juice of one lime, and some club soda. A classic beverage, popular in the American Southwest for decades, is the tequila sour—simply tequila, lemon juice, and a bit of sugar served on the rocks. The tequila sunrise, made famous by the Eagles song, not to mention its place as a hair-of-the-dog morning-after drink, is a combination of tequila, orange juice, and grenadine, which yields a tall, slightly frothed glass of red liquid at the bottom modulating toward orange at the top.

A classic Mexican way of drinking tequila is with *sangrita,* popular in tequila's birthplace of Jalisco: a sip of tequila followed by a sip of a "little blood." Today, this is usually a mixture of tomato and orange juice spiced with powdered chili and lime juice, though other recipes call for bitter Seville orange juice, grenadine syrup, salt, and powdered chili. According to Diana Kennedy, the Julia Child of Mexican cuisine, the original *sangrita* used sour pomegranate juice rather than grenadine. *Sangrita* is best made fresh, though it is also sold in jars.

SOUL

But tequila's popularity in the United States began, and has been made permanent, by one legendary cocktail: the margarita. It is hard to exaggerate the influence of this drink; for many people, it was their introduction to tequila, and for many others, it is still the only way they drink tequila. As with any famous food or drink, controversy rages over its composition and also its origin.

The first margarita is said to have been made in the late 1930s in a bar in Juárez, by a man named Danny for a woman named Margarita; or in the early 1940s in a bar on the road between Rosarito Beach and Tijuana, by a bartender named Pancho; or around the same time in the town of Tijuana itself by a man named Enrique, in honor of the actress Rita Hayworth, whose true name was Margarita Cansino. But a woman named Margaret Somes claims to have originated the drink in 1948 in her bar in Acapulco. Unless it was invented in the same year in Galveston, Texas, by a bartender named Santos for singer Peggy (Margaret) Smith, or by any number of other people in several other places in honor of a variety of other Margaritas.

Whoever invented the margarita, and there are many other versions of its origin, it entered the drink culture in Mexico sometime in the early 1940s, and it was a mixture of tequila, orange liqueur, and lime or lemon juice. The first margaritas were not blended, but were supposedly served mixed with hand-crushed or shaved ice, either in the glass or shaken in a hand shaker. It seems much more likely, however, that margaritas were originally simply poured over ice cubes and stirred, which is the way many people prefer them today—with or without a salt rim. It's not clear when or where the salt rim was added, but it's not hard to think of this as the genius touch that put the drink over the top, mixing the fruity, almost smoky intensity of tequila with the sweet-sour flavors of citrus and the shocking salinity and the earthy, coarse texture of salt with each sip (though some tequila aficionados believe that the salt detracts from margaritas made with 100 percent blue agave tequila).

The frozen margarita arrived in 1971—just in time for bell-bottoms and disco—with the invention of the frozen-margarita machine and the giant margarita glass, in the same martini shape as its predecessor but twice as large in capacity. Drinking establishments just over the border and in the American Southwest helped introduce tequila and Mexican beer to an American audience, and chain restaurants like Chevys and Chili's, along with smaller chains like the Cadillac Bar, brought Mexican food and drink to more northern and eastern states. In 1977, Jimmy Buffett recorded "Margaritaville," which became the theme song of lovers of Mexico, sun, tequila, and good times. And soon other ingredients, like strawberry puree, were being added to the margarita to give it a variety of flavors, in the tradition of the daiquiri. Unfortunately, the quality of the margarita also began to decline around this time, as sweet-and-sour mix took the place of fresh lime juice and bottled margarita mix became widely available.

Today, frozen-margarita machines can be rented for parties, and margarita mix is still everywhere. But with the development of the tequila industry and its special bottlings of premium tequilas has come a newfound respect for the liquor and an entirely new life for tequila cocktails, especially the margarita. It began with high-end drinking establishments in the United States expanding their stock of tequilas, with rows of bottles, from as many different distillers as possible, reaching to the ceiling behind the bar. Bartenders and margarita lovers found that the drink could be varied in an almost infinite number of ways by slightly altering the ingredients. Instead of using only *blanco,* the whole range of tequilas,

55

from many different purveyors and including the oldest *añejos,* were mixed with a variety of orange liqueurs instead of the usual triple sec, including Cointreau, Grand Marnier, Curaçao, and the Spanish liqueur Gran Torres, along with one, or more, "secret" ingredient such as agave nectar, to create an entire drink list of margarita choices.

With the turn of the last century, a new chapter began for tequila, both as an after-dinner drink and as a cocktail ingredient. The wider availability of premium tequilas made them the drink of choice to sip following a Latin-flavored meal, in the tradition of fine Cognacs. Tequilas became the basis for completely new drinks as bartenders turned into "mixologists," inventing cocktails using unexpected combinations and ingredients, many of them fresh, ranging from apples to zucchini. And the margarita was reinvented too, with the addition of other ingredients, including a range of fruit essences. The pomegranate margarita is one of the more popular, but the many choices include most members of the fruit family, including mango, passion fruit, and prickly pear. And of course, though the kind of tequila and orange liqueur used may differ, the lime juice is always fresh.

The margarita is one of our most popular drinks for many reasons, not least of all the fact that it is such a perfect match to Mexican food. For those who prefer not to drink beer or wine with their meal, the margarita is a fine alternative, as its fruity combination of sweetness, acidity, and salt seems to complement chile-brightened foods, from tacos to elaborate regional dishes and refined Mexico City cuisine.

The margarita is a favorite for many other reasons: the simplicity of the basic drink, served on the rocks or strained; its ability to be gussied up in festive if not somewhat outlandish ways, as a frozen slush in giant glasses with a salt rim and a wedge of lime; its seductive combination of sweetness and acidity, tropical and essential flavors; and its talent for recreation and affinity for other ingredients.

THE NEW WORLD OF TEQUILA

For such an elemental drink, tequila is a remarkably intricate subject, bringing with it a long, rich history, a wide field of varying tastes, and a confusing Spanish lexicon of both official and unofficial terms. But it is this combination of simplicity and sophistication that may be one of the keys to its growing appeal among lovers of fine liquor. Other keys are surely its uniqueness and the way in which it seems to embody the spirit of its country of origin.

High-end tequila bars, which specialize in custom cocktails and a wide variety of premium tequilas, are one of the newest trends in the United States. Tequila tastings, food and tequila pairings, and an onsite "tequilier" (the equivalent of a sommelier) may be offered as well. Because Mexico produces more than one thousand different brands of this liquor, which can vary subtly or markedly from brand to brand, tequila lends itself to many hours of pleasurable study.

In 1999, tequila was the fastest-growing distilled beverage in the world. It has become sought-after in both Japan and Europe, doubtlessly for both its New World chic and its unique flavor. The producers keep upping the ante in the category of premium tequilas, including producing single-barrel tequilas and blended-age *añejos* and *extra-añejos,* making them more and more comparable to fine Cognacs and single-malt Scotches in both complexity and price.

Like Cognac, tequila is a distilled liquor whose name is also its appellation. (Just as all tequila are mezcals but not all mezcals are tequilas, all Cognacs are brandies but not all brandies are Cognacs.) Unlike wine, tequila does not age in the bottle. Also unlike wine, it has no vintage years, as each new bottling is blended to taste the same as the previous year's. Like single-barrel whiskey, each brand of tequila has a taste unlike that of any other.

There are no subappellations for tequila, but the most obvious difference in taste is between those spirits from the valley of Tequila and those from Los Altos, the highlands. Not only does the red soil of the highlands differ from the dark soil of the valley, the climate is colder at the higher elevation of seven thousand five hundred feet. The combination of a more arid climate with lower temperatures produces smaller agaves, which need a year or two longer to mature than valley plants. All of this gives highland agaves a higher sugar content and produces sweeter tequilas than the drier ones from the lower elevations. Highland tequilas are also said to be fruitier, with notes of flowers, while valley tequilas tend toward herb and spice flavors. Some aficionados prefer highland spirits, and tequila bars often list them in a separate category on their drink list.

The latest trend in tequila is that of flavored tequilas infused with coffee, cocoa, or fruits. An agave-flavored liqueur, tequila ice cream, and margarita popsicles are a few more of the food products to capitalize on the indefinable New World taste of the blue agave.

BEBIDAS

TEQUILA COCKTAILS

Classic Margarita 64 ∞ Blood Orange Margarita 67 ∞ Tejito 68

Raspberry–Meyer Lemonade with Tequila 70 ∞ Tequila-Grapefruit Soda 71

Watermelon-Tequila Agua Fresca 72 ∞ Tequila Colada 74 ∞ Tequila Sunrise 74

Pineapple-Tequila Refresco 75 ∞ Guavarita 76 ∞ Hibiscus-Tequila Cooler 76

Mangorita 77 ∞ Mexican Greyhound 77 ∞ Cucumber and Orange Tequila Cooler 78

Very Melon Margarita 78 ∞ Bloody Maria 79 ∞ Tegroni 81

Resposado Iced Coffee 83 ∞ Amaretto-Tequila Cocktail 83

BLANCO

REPOSADO

	BLANCO		REPOSADO
AGE	Not aged	**AGE**	Three to six months
COLOR	"White," or silver (*plata,* in Spanish)	**COLOR**	Light golden
BARREL	None	**BARREL**	Oak or holm oak
PROFILE	Strong agave flavor, vegetal	**PROFILE**	Strong agave and oak flavor

TYPES OF TEQUILA

AÑEJO

EXTRA AÑEJO

AGE	Eighteen months to three years	**AGE**	Three years, plus seven to ten years
COLOR	Honey golden	**COLOR**	Dark golden
BARREL	Oak	**BARREL**	Oak, then transferred to stainless steel
PROFILE	Smoky agave and oak flavor	**PROFILE**	Deep, rich, smooth oak finish

Classic Margarita

There seems to be no consensus as to the origin of the margarita. There are many different stories about who invented it and where (see page 54). In the end, all that matters is that the margarita is here for us to enjoy. It can be served on the rocks, straight up, and with or without a salt rim. This classic version is only lightly sweet, and is crisp and refreshing.

MAKES I DRINK

Fine sea salt (optional)

1 lime wedge (optional)

1 ounce fresh lime juice

1 ounce *blanco* tequila

Dash of Cointreau liqueur

Ice cubes

If you prefer a salt-rimmed glass, put some salt in a wide, shallow bowl, rub the lime wedge around the rim of a cocktail glass, and dip the glass into the salt, shaking off any excess.

Combine the lime juice, tequila, and Cointreau in a cocktail shaker with ice and shake vigorously. Strain into a glass and serve.

Blood Orange Margarita

Blood oranges have a unique, subtle red wine essence that makes this cocktail a delightful variation from the standard lime original.

MAKES 1 DRINK

Superfine sugar

1 blood orange wedge

2 ounces fresh blood orange juice

2 ounces *blanco* tequila

1 ounce Cointreau liqueur

Ice cubes

Mint sprig

Put some sugar in a wide, shallow bowl. Run the blood orange wedge around the rim of a martini glass and reserve the wedge. Dip the rim of the glass into the sugar and shake off any excess. Set aside. Combine the orange juice, tequila, and Cointreau in a cocktail shaker with ice and shake vigorously. Strain into the prepared glass. Garnish with the reserved blood orange wedge skewered with a mint sprig.

Tejito

The mojito, the now famous cocktail, came to shore from Cuba sometime in the late 1980s but was not widely known until The Buena Vista Social Club came onto the scene in the late 1990s. The popularity of the band's music as well as the motion picture by the same name spawned an interest in Cuban culture. Sipping on a mojito seems to instantly transport one to a café in old Havana. According to legend, the origins of the mojito evolved from a drink made from sugarcane juice laced with rum that Cuban slaves drank. Using white tequila instead of rum gives the drink an earthy, slightly smoky flavor and it works deliciously well.

MAKES 1 DRINK

2 ounces fresh lime juice

1 tablespoon sugar

3 mint sprigs

Ice cubes

2 ounces *blanco* tequila

Soda water as needed

Combine the lime juice, sugar, and leaves from 2 mint sprigs in a tumbler glass. Mash with the back of a wooden spoon until the mint starts to break apart. Add the ice and tequila. Top off with soda water. Garnish with the remaining mint sprig and serve.

Raspberry–Meyer Lemonade with Tequila

Raspberry lemonade—enlivened with tequila—may be the best of all summer-porch or backyard-patio drinks on a long, hot day. Thin-skinned and fragrant, Meyer lemons give this lemonade a delightful sweetness and perfume you will not find in store-bought lemonade.

MAKES 1 DRINK

3 tablespoons fresh Meyer lemon juice

1 tablespoon sugar

About 10 fresh raspberries

1 mint sprig

Ice cubes

¼ cup water

2 ounces *blanco* tequila

Combine the lemon juice and sugar in a large glass and stir to dissolve the sugar. Add the raspberries and mint. Lightly mash the raspberries to release some of their juices. Add a few ice cubes, the water, and tequila. Give it a good stir and enjoy.

Tequila-Grapefruit Soda

Tequila mixed with Fresca is a popular drink in Mexico. This recipe uses fresh red grapefruit juice to make a similar but oh-so-much-better-tasting drink that is beyond perfect on a lazy day.

MAKES 1 DRINK

¾ cup fresh Ruby Red grapefruit juice

1 tablespoon sugar

2 ounces *blanco* tequila

Ice cubes

Soda water as needed

1 grapefruit wedge for garnish (optional)

Combine the grapefruit juice and sugar in a measuring cup and stir to dissolve the sugar. Add the tequila and stir. Pour the mixture into an ice-filled cocktail glass. Top off with soda water. Garnish with a grapefruit wedge, if desired.

Watermelon-Tequila Agua Fresca

If you've ever traveled in Mexico, you have seen them: rows of voluminous glass jars filled with "fresh waters" in a rainbow of colors. Very lightly sweet, these fruit-flavored drinks complement spicy foods and warm days. This version has just enough lime juice and tequila to brighten the flavor of the watermelon.

MAKES 6 DRINKS

1 small seedless watermelon (4 to 5 pounds)

8 cups water

1 1/2 cups sugar

1 ounce fresh lime juice

Pinch of salt

Ice cubes

6 shots *blanco* tequila

Cut the watermelon into quarters. Add about 1/2 cup of the water to the blender to keep it from clogging, and scoop the flesh of two of the watermelon quarters into the blender. Add half of the sugar and half of the lime juice and blend until smooth. Pour the puree into a 1-gallon jar or punch bowl. Add another 1/2 cup water and the remaining watermelon flesh, sugar, and lime juice to the blender and blend again. Add to the puree in the jar or bowl. Stir in the salt.

Add the remaining 7 cups water to the punch and stir well to dissolve the sugar. Ladle into 6 ice-filled glasses. Top each glass off with a shot of tequila, stir, and serve.

Tequila Colada

This is not the classic piña colada by any means. The traditional coconut syrup or cream is replaced with coconut milk, and tequila replaces the rum for a lighter-tasting drink.

MAKES 1 DRINK

4 ounces pineapple juice

1 ounce coconut milk

2 ounces *blanco* tequila

Ice cubes

Combine the pineapple juice, coconut milk, tequila, and a few ice cubes in a cocktail shaker and shake vigorously. Strain into an ice-filled glass and serve.

Tequila Sunrise

This popular tequila libation was first concocted at the Arizona Biltmore Hotel in the late 1930s or early 1940s. Fresh orange juice and *reposado* tequila elevates it to a new level.

MAKES 1 DRINK

Ice cubes

2 ounces *reposado* tequila

4 ounces fresh orange juice

¾ ounce grenadine syrup

1 maraschino or fresh cherry for garnish

Fill a tall glass three-fourths full with ice, then add the tequila and orange juice. Gradually pour the grenadine syrup into the glass. It will sink to the bottom, creating that classic sunrise look. Top with a cherry and serve.

Pineapple-Tequila Refresco

This cocktail has a smoothie-like texture and the flowery, tropical taste of pineapple. The recipe calls for a whole pineapple, so you may want to invite a few friends over to partake of this refreshingly sweet drink.

MAKES 2 DRINKS

1 ripe pineapple

2 cups water

¾ cup superfine sugar

1 lime wedge

Coarse decorating sugar

4 ounces *blanco* tequila

Ice cubes

Peel, core, and dice the pineapple. Combine half of the pineapple with 1 cup of the water and half of the superfine sugar in a blender and puree until smooth. Repeat with the remaining pineapple, water, and superfine sugar. Pour into a large pitcher and refrigerate for 1 hour to chill.

Run the lime wedge around the rims of 4 cocktail glasses and dip the rims in the coarse sugar. For each drink, combine 3 ounces pineapple mixture with 1 ounce tequila and a few ice cubes in a cocktail shaker. Shake well, strain into a sugar-rimmed glass, and serve.

Guavarita

The guava is a small tropical fruit grown widely in Mexico and prized for its intense, complex flavor. It is often made into jams, beverages, sweet confections, and a paste used much the same way as quince paste. Guava nectar is available at most supermarkets.

MAKES I DRINK

4 ounces guava nectar

2 ounces *blanco* tequila

Ice cubes

Combine the guava nectar and tequila in a cocktail shaker filled with ice and shake vigorously. Strain into a cocktail glass and serve.

Hibiscus-Tequila Cooler

The hibiscus (*jamaica* in Spanish) is a tropical flower that is used in Ayurvedic cures, teas, and even shampoos. As a deep-red iced drink, *jamaica* is popular throughout Latin America. This variation adds the light kick of tequila. Dried hibiscus flowers can be found in Latino markets and online.

MAKES 4 DRINKS

4 cups apple juice

1 ½ ounces dried hibiscus flowers

8 ounces *blanco* tequila

Ice cubes

In a medium saucepan, heat the apple juice over low heat until barely simmering. Add the hibiscus flowers, remove from the heat, and let steep for 20 minutes. Refrigerate until cool.

Strain the hibiscus mixture into a large pitcher. Discard the hibiscus flowers. For each drink, pour 1 cup of the mixture into a cocktail shaker. Add 2 ounces tequila and shake vigorously. Pour into a tall ice-filled glass and serve.

Mangorita

This variation on the margarita has a velvety smooth texture that is sure to please mango-lovers. Mango nectar is preferable to fresh mangos for its consistency of flavor and because the nectar gives the drink a lighter texture.

MAKES 1 DRINK

3 ounces mango nectar

2 ounces *blanco* tequila

1 lime wedge

Dash of Cointreau liqueur

Ice cubes

Combine the mango nectar, tequila, a squeeze of lime juice, and Cointreau in a cocktail shaker filled with ice and shake vigorously. Strain into a martini glass and serve.

Variation: *For a more sophisticated version, reserve the lime wedge used for the juice. In a small bowl, stir 2 teaspoons vanilla powder and 1/2 cup superfine sugar together. Put the mixture in a wide, shallow bowl. Rub the reserved lime wedge around the rim of a martini glass and dip the rim into the mixture, shaking off any excess. Proceed with the recipe.*

Mexican Greyhound

Sweet, sour, salty, bitter—the ingredients in this recipe create a perfect complexity of tastes. Tequila substitutes for the vodka in the classic Greyhound, and the addition of salt beautifully rounds out all the flavors of this drink.

MAKES 4 DRINKS

1 lime wedge

1/4 cup salt

Ice cubes

8 ounces (1 cup) tequila of your choice

20 ounces (2 1/2 cups) fresh grapefruit juice

Moisten the rim of 4 double old-fashioned glasses with the lime wedge. Put the salt into a wide shallow bowl and dip each glass into the salt, shaking off any excess. Fill the glasses with ice and add 2 ounces of tequila and 5 ounces grapefruit juice to each. Stir and serve.

Variation: *You may sweeten this cocktail by adding 1 teaspoon agave nectar to each drink.*

Cucumber and Orange Tequila Cooler

Cucumber and orange is a subtle and cooling flavor combination. This cooler uses cucumber-and-orange-infused water to make a truly refreshing drink.

MAKES 4 DRINKS

4 cups spring water

1 cucumber, peeled and thinly sliced

2 oranges, thinly sliced

Ice cubes

4 shots *blanco* tequila

Combine the water, cucumber, and orange slices in a glass pitcher. Let sit in the refrigerator for several hours, or overnight if possible. Strain into tall, ice-filled glasses. Add a shot of tequila to each glass, stir, and serve.

Very Melon Margarita

If you like honeydew melon, you will love this one-of-a-kind margarita. Fresh melon and melon liqueur deepen the honeydew essence.

MAKES 4 DRINKS

2 cups chopped honeydew melon

2 ounces Midori liqueur

6 ounces *blanco* tequila

1 cup crushed ice

In a blender, combine all the ingredients and blend until smooth. Pour into tall glasses and serve immediately.

78

Bloody Maria

This variation on the Bloody Mary is the perfect drink for a hearty brunch. Or, you can simply enjoy it on a hot summer afternoon.

MAKES 1 DRINK

6 ounces tomato juice

2 ounces *blanco* tequila

1 teaspoon prepared horseradish

Dash of Worcestershire sauce

Dash of Tabasco sauce

Dash of celery salt

Pinch of freshly ground pepper

Ice cubes

1 lime wedge

1 celery stalk for garnish (optional)

Combine the tomato juice, tequila, horseradish, Worcestershire, Tabasco, celery salt, and pepper in a cocktail shaker with a few ice cubes and shake vigorously. Strain into a Collins glass filled with ice. Squeeze in the lime and stir.

If using, peel the length of the celery stalk with a vegetable peeler, creating thin ribbons. Soak the ribbons in a bowl of ice water for about 1 hour. They will curl into an ornate garnish. Drop into the drink and serve.

Tegroni

This aperitif is based on the negroni, which is said to have originated in Florence, Italy, in 1919, and was named after Count Camillo Negroni. It is flavored with bitters, in this case Campari, which may be an acquired taste for some. Bitters have the uncanny ability to stimulate the appetite, making this is a perfect before-dinner drink.

MAKES I DRINK

1 ounce Campari bitters

1 ounce red vermouth

1 ounce *blanco* tequila

Ice cubes

1 strip orange zest for garnish

Combine the Campari, vermouth, tequila, and a few ice cubes in a cocktail shaker. Shake well and strain into a martini glass. Garnish with the orange zest and serve.

Reposado Iced Coffee

Reposado tequila lends an earthy flavor as well as the obvious kick to strong black coffee, with the edges rounded off by fresh cream and agave syrup.

MAKES I DRINK

6 ounces strong cold black coffee

1 ounce *reposado* tequila

1 tablespoon dark amber agave syrup

Ice cubes

1 tablespoon heavy cream

Combine the coffee, tequila, and agave syrup in a pitcher. Stir thoroughly and pour into a tall glass filled with ice. Drizzle the cream over the ice and serve.

Amaretto-Tequila Cocktail

The intense almond flavor of amaretto liqueur pairs extremely well with a *reposado* or *añejo* tequila. Although this is a cold drink, it will warm you on a cold winter's night.

MAKES I DRINK

1 ounce amaretto liqueur

2 ounces *reposado* or *añejo* tequila

Ice cubes

Almond biscotti (optional)

83

Combine the amaretto and tequila in a cocktail shaker with ice and shake vigorously. Strain into a martini glass. If you like, serve with almond biscotti.

SALADA

SAVORY TEQUILA-INSPIRED DISHES

Raw Oysters with Grapefruit-Tequila Granita 86 ⟳ Tequila-Lime Shrimp Ceviche 88
Corn Chowder with Roasted Tomatoes and Tequila 89 ⟳ Sopes 91 ⟳ Spinach Salad
with Cherries, Walnuts, and Balsamic-Agave Vinaigrette 93 ⟳ Caramelized Foie Gras
with Tequila-Orange Gastrique and Peaches 94 ⟳ Black Pepper–Encrusted New York
Steaks with Añejo Glaze 96 ⟳ Roast Chicken with Reposado Mole 97
Agave-and Mustard-Glazed Ham 98 ⟳ Tequila- and Orange-Scented Pork Ribs with
Agave Glaze 101 ⟳ Slow-Cooked Pork with Lime, Tequila, and Chile 102
Mussels with Tequila, Garlic, and Cilantro 103 ⟳ Bacon-Wrapped Monkfish with
Tequila and Chives 104 ⟳ Seared Scallops with Tequila-Cilantro Cream 107
Avocado Soup with Tequila-Poached Prawns and Caviar 108

1 cup fresh grapefruit juice

2 teaspoons light agave nectar

1 tablespoon *blanco* tequila

16 raw oysters, such as Kumamotos or Hog Island Sweetwaters, on the half shell

Freshly ground pepper for garnish

Raw Oysters with Grapefruit-Tequila Granita

The crisp acidity of the granita juxtaposed with the creamy oysters makes a wonderful combination. Salt from the oyster liquor rounds the dish out—and the tequila brings a unique depth of flavor.

MAKES 4 SERVINGS

In a small stainless-steel bowl, stir the grapefruit juice, agave nectar, and tequila together and place in the freezer. Stir every 30 minutes for 2 hours. Freeze until solid, 1 to 2 hours.

Divide the oysters among 4 small plates. Using a fork, break up and fluff the granita mixture. Put a tablespoonful on each oyster and garnish with freshly ground pepper. Serve at once.

1 pound shrimp, shelled, deveined, and coarsely chopped

1/2 cup fresh lime juice, plus more as needed

1/4 cup *blanco* tequila, plus more as needed

1/2 cup finely chopped white onion

3/4 cup diced fresh tomato

2 jalapeños, seeded and minced

1/2 teaspoon kosher salt

2 teaspoons Tabasco sauce

1 ripe avocado, peeled, pitted, and diced

2 tablespoons coarsely chopped fresh cilantro

Tequila-Lime Shrimp Ceviche

Ceviche (sometimes spelled *seviche*) is beloved throughout Latin America. This simple dish of fish "cooked" in citrus juice or vinegar is a classic first course for a Latin-flavored meal. The traditional Mexican version here uses fresh lime juice. Tequila shots, cold beer, and tortilla chips are the ideal accompaniments. Note that this dish needs to marinate overnight.

MAKES 4 SERVINGS

Combine all the ingredients except the avocado and cilantro in a nonreactive bowl. The level of liquid should just barely submerge the ingredients. If it does not, add a little more lime juice or tequila. Stir well and refrigerate overnight.

Drain off half of the liquid, stir in the avocado and cilantro, and serve.

Corn Chowder with Roasted Tomatoes and Tequila

Chowder makes a great light lunch or hearty first course. This one is thick and creamy, thanks to the natural starches in the fresh corn kernels. Stir in a little tequila just before serving to add its vibrant flavor to this colorful dish.

MAKES 8 FIRST-COURSE OR 4 MAIN-COURSE SERVINGS

4 strips thick bacon, diced

1 yellow onion, diced

1 large carrot, peeled and diced

2 celery stalks, diced

4 cups rich chicken stock

8 ounces Yukon gold potatoes, peeled and diced (keep in water until needed)

2 ears fresh corn, husked

8 ounces large cherry tomatoes, halved

Dash of olive oil

Salt and freshly ground pepper to taste

1/2 cup *blanco* tequila

Chopped fresh cilantro for garnish

Chopped green onion for garnish

Sauté the bacon over medium heat in a medium stockpot until crisp. Transfer to paper towels to drain. Pour off all but 2 tablespoons of the bacon fat from the pot and add the onion, carrot, and celery, stirring until the celery turns bright green, about 3 minutes. Add the stock and potatoes. Simmer over medium-low heat until the potatoes are tender but not falling apart, 10 to 15 minutes. Meanwhile, cut the corn kernels off their cobs and scrape as much of the starchy juices from each cob as possible. Stir the corn and juices into the pot and reduce the heat to low.

For the roasted tomatoes: Preheat the oven to 400°F. Line a baking sheet with parchment paper. Put the tomatoes in a bowl, add a generous dash of olive oil, and season with salt and pepper. Transfer to the prepared pan and roast for 25 minutes, or until the tomatoes have wrinkled and shrunk. Remove from the oven and set aside.

To finish the soup, increase the heat to medium and season to taste with salt and pepper. Add the tequila, stir, and ladle into warmed bowls. Garnish with the roasted tomatoes, cilantro, and green onion. Serve at once.

89

SOPES

1 1/2 cups masa harina

1/8 teaspoon baking powder

1/8 teaspoon salt

1/3 cup nonhydrogenated
vegetable shortening or lard

About 3/4 cup warm water

FILLINGS

1 cup Slow-Cooked Pork with
Lime, Tequila, and Chile
(page 102)

1/2 cup pico de gallo salsa

1/2 cup crumbled queso fresco
or feta cheese

Sour cream as needed

1 large red radish, thinly sliced

Sopes

Sopes are traditional Mexican appetizers made from fresh masa or masa harina, the same dough or corn flour used in making tortillas. Shaped into small boats, they are filled with meats, cheeses, or salsa and are the ideal complement to a fine *añejo* tequila.

MAKES ABOUT I DOZEN SOPES

For the sopes: Preheat the oven to 375°F. Line a baking sheet with parchment paper. In a large bowl, stir the masa harina, baking powder, and salt together. Add the shortening and blend with a pastry blender until the mixture resembles coarse crumbs. Gradually add the warm water until the mixture has a soft dough consistency. Knead for a minute or so, then form into balls about the size of a small walnut, about 1 1/2 tablespoons per ball. Form the balls into small cup shapes. They don't need to be perfect, as long as there are no holes in them. The thinner the walls and base of the cups are, the more delicate the end result will be.

Transfer the cups to the prepared sheet and bake for 30 minutes, or just until the edges start to brown. Fill the cups with any combination of the fillings, garnish with the sour cream and radish slices, and serve at once.

BALSAMIC-AGAVE VINAIGRETTE

1 tablespoon minced shallot

¼ cup aged balsamic vinegar

2 tablespoons light agave nectar

1 tablespoon stone-ground mustard

2 tablespoons walnut oil

½ cup extra-virgin olive oil

Salt and freshly ground pepper to taste

1 cup fresh Bing cherries, pitted and halved, or ½ cup dried pitted cherries

¾ cup walnuts, toasted and coarsely chopped

6 cups washed baby spinach

Spinach Salad with Cherries, Walnuts, and Balsamic-Agave Vinaigrette

Agave nectar is used in this recipe to round out the acidity of the balsamic vinegar and to bring a silky texture to the dressing. Reserve the remaining portion of this vinaigrette to use on any salad or as a marinade for grilled vegetables.

MAKES 4 SERVINGS

For the vinaigrette: In a blender, puree the shallot, balsamic vinegar, agave nectar, mustard, and walnut oil. Gradually whisk in the olive oil to make an emulsion. Season with salt and pepper.

In a large bowl, toss the cherries, walnuts, and spinach with ½ cup of the vinaigrette. Refrigerate the remaining vinaigrette for other salads. Divide the salad among 4 plates and serve immediately.

Variation: *Sprinkle ½ cup crumbled Gorgonzola cheese over the salad just before serving.*

½ cup light agave nectar

Juice of 1 orange

¼ cup Champagne vinegar

1 tablespoon *blanco* tequila

1 teaspoon grated orange zest

2 large peaches, peeled, pitted, and sliced

1 thyme sprig

Four 2½-ounce pieces foie gras

Salt and freshly ground pepper to taste

4 slices brioche, cut slightly smaller than the foie gras pieces, toasted

Caramelized Foie Gras with Tequila-Orange Gastrique and Peaches

The tequila in this gastrique recipe adds a unique aged characteristic that complements the richness of the foie gras. Any stone fruit can be used in place of peaches.

MAKES 4 SERVINGS

For the gastrique: In a heavy saucepan, bring the agave nectar, orange juice, and vinegar to a boil. Reduce the heat to low and simmer until syrupy, about 4 minutes. Remove from the heat and stir in the tequila and orange zest. Set aside.

In a medium bowl, toss the peaches and the thyme sprig with 2 tablespoons of the gastrique. In a large sauté pan, cook the peach mixture over high heat until the peaches are caramelized on both sides, about 3 minutes. Remove from the heat and discard the thyme sprig.

Season the foie gras generously with salt and pepper. Heat a large nonstick skillet over medium heat for 4 minutes. Add 2 pieces of the foie gras and sear until caramelized, 2 to 3 minutes on each side. Transfer to a plate and repeat with the remaining foie gras.

Divide the peaches among 4 plates. Place each piece of seared foie gras on a piece of toasted brioche and set on top of the peaches. Drizzle with the remaining gastrique.

94

Black Pepper–Encrusted
New York Steaks with Añejo Glaze

Two 8-ounce New York steaks, preferably prime beef

1 tablespoon freshly ground pepper

Gray sea salt or kosher salt to taste

1 teaspoon canola oil

¼ cup *añejo* tequila

1 cup rich beef stock

Use prime New York steaks if you can find them. Their flavor and tenderness are worth the extra cost. Using a heavy cast-iron skillet will help to give the meat a crisp crust. Although *añejo* tequila is not absolutely necessary for this recipe, it's a good match for top-quality steaks. Serve with your favorite sides, such as French fries, roasted or baked potatoes, and creamed spinach.

MAKES 2 SERVINGS

Coat the steaks with the pepper on both sides and let stand at room temperature for about 1 hour. Season with the salt, then gently press the salt and pepper into the steaks.

Heat a large cast-iron skillet over high heat until very hot, then add the oil. Swirl to coat, then add the steaks. Let cook without disturbing for about 2 minutes, or until the steaks are dark brown on the bottom. (You can check the color by peeking under a corner of a steak without moving it.) Turn the steaks over and continue cooking for another minute or two for medium rare. Transfer to a warmed platter or plates and let rest for at least 5 minutes, but not more than 10.

Place the skillet over medium-high heat. Standing back, add the tequila and beef stock; the tequila will flame up. When the flames subside stir to scrape up the browned bits from the bottom of the pan. Reduce the heat to medium and cook to reduce to about ¼ cup sauce. Divide the sauce equally over the steaks and serve.

96

1 small (about 3 pounds) roasting chicken

4 oregano or marjoram sprigs

1 tablespoon kosher salt

2 teaspoons freshly ground pepper

Olive oil for brushing

1/2 cup water

2 tablespoons mole paste

1/2 cup *reposado* tequila

Roast Chicken with Reposado Mole

Both the agave plant and the cacao bean were sacred to the ancient Mesoamericans, and used ceremoniously as well as for nourishment. Here, these two flavors are combined in a delectable poultry dish. Be sure to salt the chicken at least twenty-four hours in advance; it really does yield a more tender and flavorful meat.

MAKES 2 SERVINGS

Remove the giblets and any large pieces of fat from the chicken. Rinse and thoroughly pat the outside and inside of the chicken dry. Slide a finger under the skin over the breast without tearing the skin. Carefully place the oregano sprigs under the skin and season the bird on the outside and inside with the salt and pepper. Let sit uncovered in the refrigerator for at least 24 hours or up to 3 days. Before roasting, let the bird sit at room temperature for an hour or so.

Adjust a rack to the middle of the oven and preheat to 500°F. Brush the inside of a large ovenproof stainless-steel skillet with a little oil. Heat the skillet over high heat until almost smoking. Add the chicken, breast-side up. Place in the oven and roast for about 15 minutes, then reduce the temperature to 475°F and roast for another 15 minutes. Turn the bird breast-side down and roast for 10 minutes, then turn it breast-side up again for the last 10 minutes to recrisp the skin.

Remove from the oven and let the chicken rest for 10 to 15 minutes. Transfer the bird to a carving board. Carve the bird and divide it among warmed plates.

Return the skillet to the stove top over medium-high heat. Add the water and mole paste, stirring to dissolve the mole and scrape up the browned bits from the bottom of the pan. Turn off the heat and, standing back, add the tequila; it will flame up. Shake the pan until the flames have subsided. Cook the liquid over medium heat to reduce until slightly thickened. Taste and adjust the seasoning. Pour the sauce over the chicken and serve at once.

One 16- to 20-pound whole
bone-in smoked ham

40 to 50 cloves

1 1/2 cups dry sherry, plus
1/2 cup for glaze

2 cups light agave nectar

5 tablespoons Dijon mustard

Agave- and Mustard-Glazed Ham

This whole bone-in smoked ham will feed a large crowd of up to twenty people. But you may want to keep the head count a bit lower, since the leftovers keep for at least another week refrigerated and are perfect for sandwiches, salads, and soups, not to mention breakfast. You can even make a rich, smoky stock from the bone.

MAKES ABOUT 20 SERVINGS

Preheat the oven to 300°F. Set the ham on a heavy cutting board. With a sharp knife, trim off the skin, leaving as much of the fat intact as possible. Score the fat in a crisscross pattern about 1/2 inch deep and 2 inches apart, creating diamond shapes. Press the pointed end of a clove into the center of each diamond. Don't concern yourself with the underside of the ham; it will not be visible.

Place the ham in a large roasting pan and bake in the oven for 4 to 5 hours, or until an instant-read thermometer inserted in the center of the meat but not touching bone registers 150°F. Baste with some of the 1 1/2 cups sherry every 20 minutes.

Meanwhile, in a medium saucepan, combine the agave nectar, mustard, and the 1/2 cup sherry. Simmer over medium heat until reduced by about a third. Remove from the heat and let cool.

Using a large pastry brush, coat the ham with glaze and bake for 20 more minutes. Remove from the oven and transfer the ham to a carving board. Let the ham rest for at least 20 minutes before carving.

Carve the ham, divide among warmed plates, and serve with your favorite side dishes.

MARINADE

Grated zest and juice of
2 oranges

4 cloves garlic, minced

1 cup *reposado* tequila

½ cup seasoned rice wine
vinegar

2 tablespoons kosher salt

4 pounds baby back ribs

AGAVE GLAZE

1 cup tomato paste

1 cup dark agave nectar

⅓ cup seasoned rice wine
vinegar

5 chipotle chiles en adobo,
seeded, 2 tablespoons adobo
sauce

1 tablespoon kosher salt

2 garlic cloves, minced

Chopped fresh cilantro for
garnish

Tequila- and Orange-Scented Pork Ribs with Agave Glaze

These ribs have a falling-off-the-bone barbecued tenderness, but their flavor is brighter, thanks to the orange essence, with a subtle smokiness added by the chipotle chiles and the *reposado* tequila.

MAKES 4 SERVINGS

For the marinade: Combine all the marinade ingredients in a bowl and stir until the salt is dissolved. Cut the rib racks in half and place in a 9-by-13-inch baking dish. Pour the marinade over the ribs and refrigerate for at least 2 hours, occasionally turning the ribs to make sure they are evenly coated.

For the glaze: Combine all the glaze ingredients in a food processor. Process until smooth and transfer to a bowl. Set aside.

Preheat the oven to 400°F. Line a baking sheet with aluminum foil. Place the rib racks on the prepared pan without overlapping. Discard the marinade. Bake for 20 minutes, then reduce the oven temperature to 275°F and bake for 2 more hours, or until very tender. During the last 20 minutes of baking, brush the ribs evenly with the glaze every 5 minutes.

Remove from the oven and transfer to a warmed platter. Garnish with cilantro and serve with any remaining glaze on the side.

1 cup *blanco* tequila

¼ cup distilled white vinegar

2 teaspoons grated lime zest

Juice of 2 limes

1½ tablespoons kosher salt

2 tablespoons powdered chile

1 bay leaf

3 cloves garlic, coarsely chopped

One 3-pound boneless pork shoulder

Slow-Cooked Pork with Lime, Tequila, and Chile

Fatty cuts of meat, like pork shoulder, benefit from long, slow cooking. The result is luscious, tender, and foolproof. Use this pork to make pulled pork sandwiches, soups, or stews. You can also combine it with cooked beans or rice to make tacos or eat it all on its own.

MAKES 6 SERVINGS

In a large glass or other nonreactive bowl, combine all the ingredients except the pork. Stir to dissolve the salt, then place the pork in the bowl and turn to coat. Cover and refrigerate for at least 3 hours, turning the pork occasionally.

Preheat the oven to 225°F. Adjust a rack in the center of the oven. Line a baking sheet with parchment paper.

Remove the pork from the marinade and discard the marinade. Pat the pork dry and place on the prepared pan. Bake for about 8 hours, or until the meat is fork-tender. Remove from the oven and let cool for about 20 minutes. The pork will have shrunk considerably.

To serve, simply pull it apart and chop into chunks. Let any leftovers cool completely, cover, and refrigerate for up to 5 days.

6 tablespoons unsalted butter

4 cloves garlic, minced

2 tablespoons minced shallots

2 pounds mussels, scrubbed and debearded

2 tablespoons fresh lime juice

¼ cup *blanco* tequila

1 teaspoon red pepper flakes (optional)

¼ cup minced fresh cilantro

Mussels with Tequila, Garlic, and Cilantro

This dish is a breeze to prepare and should always be made just before serving. Meaty, sweet mussels lend themselves to bold flavors, and here, tequila, garlic, lime, and cilantro add brightness and excitement to a classic dish. Serve with crusty bread for dipping.

MAKES 4 SERVINGS

In a wide, deep saucepan, melt the butter over medium heat. Add the garlic and shallots and sauté until the shallots are translucent, about 3 minutes. Add the mussels, lime juice, tequila, and pepper flakes, if using. Cover the pan and continue cooking, shaking the pan from time to time, for 5 to 6 minutes, or until the mussels have opened. Add the cilantro and shake the pan a few more times to distribute the ingredients. Remove from the heat and discard any mussels that have not opened. Divide equally among 4 bowls and serve.

Four 6-ounce monkfish fillets

4 slices thick bacon

Salt and freshly ground pepper
to taste

3 tablespoons unsalted butter

½ cup *añejo* tequila

Sautéed spinach, arugula, or
chard for serving

1 bunch chives, finely snipped,
for garnish

Bacon-Wrapped Monkfish with Tequila and Chives

Monkfish has been called the poor man's lobster, and although it is similar in flavor, it is more tender and easier to prepare. The bacon adds richness in addition to balancing the tequila's sharpness. Take care when deglazing the pan with tequila—the word *pyrotechnics* comes to mind—remember to stand back.

MAKES 4 SERVINGS

Preheat the oven to 400°F. Using a small, sharp knife, remove any slimy tissue from the fillets. Wrap a slice of bacon around each fillet, stretching the bacon so that it will shrink around the fish when cooked. Secure the bacon with a toothpick. Season with salt and pepper.

In an ovenproof stainless-steel skillet, melt the butter over medium-low to medium heat. Add the fillets and brown on both sides, about 7 minutes per side. Do not increase the heat to speed things up; you need only enough heat to brown the bacon and fillets, not to cook them through. Transfer the skillet to the oven to finish cooking, 10 to 15 minutes. The fillets should be quite firm to the touch and opaque throughout when done.

Using an oven mitt (the handle will be very hot), return the skillet to the stove top. Transfer the fish to a warmed platter. Place the pan over medium-high heat, stand far back, and add the tequila to the pan; it will flame up. When the flames subside, stir to scrape up the browned bits from the bottom of the pan. This will be your sauce.

Make a bed of sautéed greens on each of 4 warmed plates and top each with a fish fillet. Pour the sauce over and around the fish. Sprinkle with chives and serve immediately.

½ cup heavy cream

½ cup chopped fresh cilantro, plus 4 sprigs for garnish

12 large sea scallops

Salt and freshly ground white pepper to taste

1 tablespoon olive oil

1 tablespoon unsalted butter

⅓ cup *reposado* tequila

½ cup shelled green peas

Seared Scallops with Tequila-Cilantro Cream

Day boat, or diver, scallops are of higher quality than conventional sea scallops. Gathered by hand from the ocean floor from New Jersey all the way into Canada, they have a firmer texture and better flavor that is a perfect match for a fine *reposado* tequila.

MAKES 4 SERVINGS

Pour the cream and chopped cilantro into a blender and blend until fairly smooth. Set aside.

Remove any small muscular membranes on the side of the scallops. Pat dry and season with a little salt and pepper. Heat a 10-inch stainless-steel skillet over medium-high heat. Add the oil and then the butter. Swirl the pan around to distribute the mixture. Quickly and carefully add the scallops one at a time and let them brown undisturbed, about 1 minute. Peek under one or two to make sure they're ready, then, using tongs, turn them over and brown the other side for another minute. Be careful not to overcook them.

Transfer the scallops to a warmed plate. To the same pan, over medium heat, add the cream mixture, tequila, and peas. Cook to reduce until thickened, 1 to 2 minutes. Season to taste with salt and pepper. Divide among 4 warmed small plates. Place 3 scallops on the sauce on each plate and garnish with a cilantro sprig. Serve at once.

3 ½ cups chicken stock

1 cup *blanco* tequila

1 teaspoon coriander seeds,
toasted and lightly crushed

12 prawns (jumbo shrimp)

2 large ripe avocados, peeled
and pitted

½ cup heavy cream

1 teaspoon fresh lemon juice

1 ½ teaspoons sherry vinegar

Salt to taste

¼ cup crème fraîche

1 ounce osetra caviar

Avocado Soup with Tequila-Poached Prawns and Caviar

The crunch of a perfectly poached prawn is a great contrast to the silky texture of this soup. There is enough acid in this recipe to keep the avocados from oxidizing, but it should be made and served immediately.

MAKES 4 SERVINGS

In a small saucepan, combine 2 cups of the chicken stock, the tequila, and coriander seeds. Bring to a simmer over medium heat. Add the prawns and cook until pink, about 3 minutes. Remove from the heat.

In a blender, puree the avocados, the remaining 1 ½ cups chicken stock, the cream, lemon, and sherry vinegar until smooth. Season with salt. In a medium saucepan over low heat, heat the soup just to warm.

Divide the soup among 4 shallow bowls and garnish each with 1 tablespoon crème fraîche, 3 prawns, and 1 ½ teaspoons caviar.

DULCE

TEQUILA AND AGAVE DESSERTS

Agave Orange Cardamom Caramels with Fleur de Sel 112 ∾ Agave-Pistachio Florentines with Green Tea Powder 114 ∾ Tapioca Pudding with Tequila and Strawberries 116 ∾ Banana Napoleons with Agave Caramel 118 ∾ Blood-Orange Panna Cotta with Agave-Roasted Mangos 121 ∾ Pátzcuaro Hot Chocolate 122

Zest of 1 orange cut into wide strips, plus grated orange zest for garnish

1 ½ cups heavy cream

¾ teaspoon ground cardamom

⅓ cup unsalted butter

1 teaspoon fleur de sel, plus more for garnish

1 ½ cups sugar

1 cup light agave nectar

Agave Orange Cardamom Caramels with Fleur de Sel

Unless you have experienced this slightly salty confection, the addition of salt may seem odd, but after just one taste you will see that it balances the sweetness of the agave nectar perfectly. The additions of orange and cardamom give these caramels a unique essence. If you are not familiar with candy making, there are two things you should know: (1) Boiling syrup is potentially hazardous. If it comes into contact with skin it tends to stick and burn; (2) You must cook the syrup to exactly the required temperature to ensure the necessary caramel consistency.

MAKES 64 CARAMELS

Butter an 8-inch square baking pan and line the bottom with a piece of parchment paper. Set aside. Combine the orange strips , cream, cardamom, butter, and the 1 teaspoon fleur de sel in a small saucepan. Place over low heat to barely simmer while you prepare the syrup.

In a medium saucepan, combine the sugar and agave nectar. Cook over medium heat, stirring often, until the sugar is dissolved. Continue heating without stirring until the syrup is a dark honey color. Briefly remove the syrup from the stove while you strain the cream mixture into a pourable measuring cup. Return the syrup to medium heat and gradually stir the cream mixture into the syrup. Take care, as the mixture will bubble up. Bring to boil and cook, stirring frequently, until a candy thermometer registers 280°F (about 15 minutes). Pour into the prepared pan. Very lightly sprinkle with fleur de sel and grated orange zest to garnish. Let cool before cutting into 1-inch squares.

4 tablespoons salted butter

½ cup packed light brown sugar

¼ cup light agave nectar

⅓ cup all-purpose flour

½ cup coarsely chopped pistachio nuts

Matcha (green tea powder) for dusting

Agave-Pistachio Florentines with Green Tea Powder

These cookies are dusted with matcha, a very fine powder made from green tea, that complements the pistachio and caramel flavors of these delicate confections. Matcha is available at most natural foods stores or online.

MAKES TWO DOZEN

Preheat the oven to 350°F. Line a baking sheet with parchment paper. In a small saucepan, combine the butter, brown sugar, and agave nectar and cook over medium-low heat, stirring occasionally, until smooth. Remove from the heat and stir in the flour and pistachios. Set aside and let cool.

Roll about 2 teaspoons batter into a ball and place on the prepared sheet. Lightly flatten. Repeat to make 3 more rounds about 6 inches apart. Bake in the center of the oven for about 7 minutes, or until golden brown. Remove from the oven and let cool for a minute or two, just until firm enough to pick up with a thin spatula. Drape cookies over a rolling pin or wine bottle to give them an elegant curve. Repeat with the remaining batter, working one sheet at a time. Using a small sieve, very lightly dust the cookies with matcha. Store in an airtight container.

1/3 cup small pearl tapioca (not instant or quick)

3 cups whole milk

1/3 cup sugar

1/4 teaspoon salt

3 large eggs, separated

1 teaspoon vanilla extract

1 tablespoon unsalted butter

2 cups fresh strawberries, hulled and sliced

1/4 cup *reposado* tequila

116

Tapioca Pudding with Tequila and Strawberries

You don't often see tapioca on restaurant menus these days, which is a shame. As far as puddings go, tapioca mixed with fresh fruit is a divinely refreshing dessert that is also a true comfort food.

MAKES 4 SERVINGS

Combine the tapioca and 1 cup of the milk in a heavy, medium saucepan. Let soak for 1 hour. Add the remaining 2 cups milk, the sugar, and salt. Whisk in the egg yolks. Bring to a simmer over medium heat, stirring constantly. Reduce the heat to low and continue simmering for 25 minutes, or until the tapioca pearls are translucent. Be careful not to overcook or scorch. Remove from the heat and stir in the vanilla. Let cool completely.

In a large bowl, beat the egg whites until soft peaks form. Carefully fold into the cooled tapioca.

In a large sauté pan, melt the butter over medium-high heat. Add the strawberries and cook until the berries begin to soften. Remove from the heat and stir in the tequila. Return to the heat and cook until most of the liquid has evaporated. Remove from the heat and let cool completely.

To assemble, layer the strawberries and tapioca in tall glasses. Refrigerate until ready to serve.

1 sheet frozen puff pastry, thawed in refrigerator

4 ripe bananas, peeled

4 tablespoons unsalted butter

$\frac{1}{3}$ cup *añejo* tequila

$\frac{3}{4}$ cup dark amber agave nectar

1 pint dolce de leche or vanilla bean ice cream

Banana Napoleons with Agave Caramel

The crisp, buttery puff pastry and tender fried bananas offer a scrumptious textural contrast in this dessert, sweetened with an agave-tequila caramel. This pastry is relatively quick and easy to make.

MAKES 4 SERVINGS

Preheat the oven to 400°F. Line a baking sheet with parchment paper. On a floured surface, roll the puff pastry to a $\frac{1}{8}$-inch thickness. With a sharp knife or pastry cutter, cut into twelve 3-inch squares and transfer to the prepared pan. Cover with another piece of parchment and place another baking sheet on top. Bake in the center of the oven for about 25 minutes, or until golden brown. Transfer the squares to a wire rack and let cool.

Peel and slice the bananas lengthwise, and then slice each half into thirds. Melt the butter in a large nonstick sauté pan over medium-high heat. Add the bananas all at once, and cook until browned on the bottom. Turn the bananas over. Add the tequila and agave nectar and reduce the heat to medium. Cook until the sauce has reduced by two-thirds and has thickened to a caramel-like consistency.

Place a puff pastry square on each plate, and top with 2 banana slices. Repeat to make 3 layers. Drizzle with the banana sauce and top with a scoop of ice cream.

PANNA COTTA

1 envelope unflavored gelatin

1/3 cup skim milk

2 1/2 cups heavy cream

1/2 cup sugar

1 vanilla bean halved lengthwise

Zest of 1 blood orange, cut into wide strips

Tiny pinch of salt

2 mangos peeled and cut from pit

1/3 cup *blanco* tequila

1/2 cup light agave nectar

1 cup blood orange juice

4 thin slices blood orange for garnish (optional)

Blood Orange Panna Cotta with Agave-Roasted Mangos

Panna cotta is a traditional Italian dessert from the Piedmont region of northern Italy. The smooth, delicate "cooked cream" is a beautiful contrast with the deep red sauce and brilliant orange mangos.

MAKES 4 SERVINGS

For the panna cotta: In a small bowl, combine the gelatin and milk; stir and set aside. In a medium saucepan, combine the cream, sugar, vanilla bean, orange zest, and salt. Simmer over medium-low heat for about 10 minutes, add the gelatin mixture and stir until the gelatin is dissolved. Remove the zest and vanilla bean and pour the mixture into six 6-ounce ramekins. Refrigerate for about 5 hours, or until completely set.

Preheat the oven to 400°F. Line a baking sheet with parchment paper. Cut the mangos into 1/2-inch-thick slices and place in a bowl with the tequila and 1/4 cup of the agave nectar. Let stand for 30 minutes. Place the mango slices on the prepared pan and roast for 10 minutes. Remove from oven and let cool without disturbing the mango.

In a small saucepan, combine the blood orange juice and the remaining 1/4 cup agave nectar. Simmer over low heat until reduced by about two-thirds. Remove from the heat and let cool.

Briefly dip the bottom of each ramekin in hot water and run a knife around the inside edge of the panna cotta. Unmold onto a dessert plate. Serve with the roasted mango slices and the blood orange sauce. Garnish with a slice of blood orange, if desired.

4 cups whole milk

¼ cup sugar

Grated zest of 1 orange

1 teaspoon ground cinnamon

4 to 5 cloves

Generous pinch of red pepper flakes

½ cup unsweetened cocoa powder

8 ounces bittersweet chocolate chips

9 ounces *añejo* tequila

6 tablespoons whipped cream

Pátzcuaro Hot Chocolate

This comforting yet inspiriting beverage is featured at JAR, Suzanne Tracht's L.A. restaurant. Named after the famous mountain town in Michoacan state, this drink is a warming blend of chocolate, tequila, and spices.

MAKES 6 DRINKS

In a medium saucepan, combine the milk, sugar, orange zest, cinnamon, cloves, and red pepper flakes. Bring to a simmer over low heat (do not boil) and whisk in the cocoa powder until completely blended. Pour the hot mixture over the chocolate chips in a bowl. Let stand for 3 to 4 minutes to let the chips melt, then stir to combine. Strain through a sieve to remove the spices. Return to the saucepan and warm over low heat.

Pour 1½ ounces of tequila into each of 6 glasses. Pour some hot chocolate over the tequila in each glass and stir. Top each glass with a spoonful of whipped cream.

AGAVE A desert succulent indigenous to Mexico, the Southwest United States, Central America, and the Caribbean basin. There are hundreds of species (Mexico alone is said to have at least 125), including the blue agave, from which tequila is made.

AGAVE TEQUILANA WEBER The botanical name of the blue agave; *agave* comes from Greek, meaning "admirable" or "noble"; *tequilana* is the place of origin; and Weber was the name of the botanist who classified the plant early in the twentieth century. Blue agave is indigenous to the region of Tequila, and the essential ingredient in tequila.

AGUAMIEL "Honey water," the juice of the agave plant, used to make pulque.

BLUE AGAVE See *Agave tequilana Weber.*

CABALLITO ("pony") The traditional tall, narrow glass for serving a shot of tequila; it is supposedly modeled after the bulls' horns and is still used for tasting tequila at some factories.

COA The long-handled tool used to harvest agave hearts.

JALISCO The Mexican state where tequila originated. It is also the birthplace of the *charros* (Mexican cowboys) and of mariachi music. Jalisco is located about halfway down the outward-curving western coast of Mexico; its capital is Guadalajara.

JIMA The underground stem, or rhizome, of the blue agave; also the act of cutting the agave plant free of its underground stem and cutting the leaves away from the heart.

JIMADOR The worker who harvests the heart of the blue agave.

124 A Tequila Glossary

JOSÉ CUERVO The first recorded producer of tequila. The company he founded in 1795 is still in operation.

MAGUEY The Spanish word for *agave* (derived from a Caribbean-Indian word).

MAYAHUEL The Mexican goddess of the agave plant.

MEZCAL (or *mexcal*; in English, *mescal*) One of the names for agave plants in general; also a distilled liquor made from agave. The name comes from the Náhuatl word *metl* or *mexametl*. (Náhuatl was the language of the Aztecs and several other Indian groups, including the Mexicas, who were part of the Aztec Triple Alliance.) Mezcal is made from one of eight different varieties of agave, not including the blue agave. The *piñas* are baked underground in a charcoal-fired pit kiln, which gives the liquor a smoky flavor. Mezcal is darker in color and more assertive in taste than tequila; some of the lesser mezcals contain a worm that feeds on the agave plant.

MIXTO "Mixed" tequila, which is made from a minimum of 51 percent blue agave sugar combined with another kind of sugar, usually cane.

MOSTO Spanish for "must," the juice of the cooked agave heart.

NÁHUATL The language of the Aztecs and several other Indian groups of Mexico's central plateau; many of the most common Mexican-Spanish words, such as *chile*, *chocolate*, *guacamole*, *mezcal*, *mole*, *tamal*, and *tomate*, are Náhuatl.

PENCAS The leaves of the agave plant.

PIÑA The heart of the blue agave, which is cooked to make tequila. It is so called because it resembles a pine-cone once its leaves are cut off.

PREMIUM TEQUILA Usually refers to 100 percent blue agave tequila, or tequila that is otherwise superior to a *blanco mixto* in some way, such as age or limited production.

PULQUE The fermented juice of one of three varieties of agave, not including the blue agave. Pulque is a fermented but not distilled liquor that predates the Conquistadors. A ritual drink in ancient times, it is still produced and is served in taverns called *pulquerías*.

PURE TEQUILA Tequila made from 100 percent blue agave. True only of tequila whose labels state "100 percent agave"; otherwise, tequila is made of at least 51 percent blue agave mixed with one or more other sugars, usually cane (see *mixto*).

TEQUILA (1) Among many other possible derivations, a word thought to come from the Náhuatl words *tequitl*, "job" or "trade," and *tlan*, "place": "a place of work" (presumably, the harvesting of agave plants to make pulque); (2) the name of a town, a valley, and an extinct volcano in Jalisco state; (3) a liquor made from blue agave and produced in the state of Jalisco and the bordering areas of the states of Michoacán, Guanajuato, Colima, and Nayarit, and a section of the state of Tamaulipas.

Index

Agave. *See also individual recipes*
    appearance of, 15
    goddess of, 29, 35, 49
    nectar, 21
    propagation methods for, 49–50
    ripening of, 19
    sacredness of, 19
    species of, 15, 31
    uses for, 20
Agua Fresca, Watermelon-Tequila, 72
Amaretto-Tequila Cocktail, 83
Avocado Soup with Tequila-Poached Prawns and Caviar, 108
Aztecs, 23, 28, 29

Banana Napoleons with Agave Caramel, 118
Beef
    Black Pepper–Encrusted New York Steaks with
        Añejo Glaze, 96

Campari
    Tegroni, 81
Caramels, Agave Orange Cardamom, with Fleur de Sel, 112
Caviar, Avocado Soup with Tequila-Poached Prawns and, 108
Chicken, Roast, with Reposado Mole, 97
Chocolate, Pátzcuaro Hot, 122
Cocktails
    Amaretto-Tequila Cocktail, 83
    Blood Orange Margarita, 67
    Bloody Maria, 79
    Classic Margarita, 64
    Cucumber and Orange Tequila Cooler, 78
    Guavarita, 76
    Hibiscus-Tequila Cooler, 76
    Mangorita, 77
    Mexican Greyhound, 77
    Pineapple-Tequila Refresco, 75

Raspberry–Meyer Lemonade with Tequila, 70
Reposado Iced Coffee, 83
Tegroni, 81
Tejito, 68
Tequila Colada, 74
Tequila-Grapefruit Soda, 71
Tequila Sunrise, 74
Very Melon Margarita, 78
Watermelon-Tequila Agua Fresca, 72
Coffee, Reposado Iced, 83
Corn Chowder with Roasted Tomatoes and Tequila, 89
Cucumber and Orange Tequila Cooler, 78

Florentines, Agave-Pistachio, with Green Tea Powder, 114
Foie Gras, Caramelized, with Tequila-Orange Gastrique
    and Peaches, 94

Granita, Grapefruit-Tequila, Raw Oysters with, 86
Grapefruit
    Mexican Greyhound, 77
    Raw Oysters with Grapefruit-Tequila Granita, 86
    Tequila-Grapefruit Soda, 71
Guavarita, 76

Ham, Agave- and Mustard-Glazed, 98
Hibiscus-Tequila Cooler, 76
Hot Chocolate, Pátzcuaro, 122

Lemonade, Raspberry–Meyer, with Tequila, 70
Limes
    Classic Margarita, 64
    Slow-Cooked Pork with Lime, Tequila, and Chile, 102
    Tejito, 68
    Tequila-Lime Shrimp Ceviche, 88

Mangos
    Blood Orange Panna Cotta with Agave-Roasted
        Mangos, 121
    Mangorita, 77
Margaritas, 54–57, 64, 67, 76–78
Mayahuel, 29, 49
Mayans, 26, 28

126

Melons
    Very Melon Margarita, 78
    Watermelon-Tequila Agua Fresca, 72
Mezcal, 20, 30–31
Monkfish, Bacon-Wrapped, with Tequila and Chives, 104
Mussels with Tequila, Garlic, and Cilantro, 103

Napoleons, Banana, with Agave Caramel, 118

Oranges
    Agave Orange Cardamom Caramels with
      Fleur de Sel, 112
    Blood Orange Margarita, 67
    Blood Orange Panna Cotta with Agave-Roasted
      Mangos, 121
    Caramelized Foie Gras with Tequila-Orange Gastrique
      and Peaches, 94
    Cucumber and Orange Tequila Cooler, 78
    Tequila- and Orange-Scented Pork Ribs with Agave
      Glaze, 101
    Tequila Sunrise, 74
Oysters, Raw, with Grapefruit-Tequila Granita, 86

Panna Cotta, Blood Orange, with Agave-Roasted Mangos, 121
Pátzcuaro Hot Chocolate, 122
Peaches, Caramelized Foie Gras with Tequila-Orange
    Gastrique and, 94
Pineapple
    Pineapple-Tequila Refresco, 75
    Tequila Colada, 74
Pork
    Slow-Cooked Pork with Lime, Tequila, and Chile, 102
    Sopes, 91
    Tequila- and Orange-Scented Pork Ribs with Agave
      Glaze, 101
Prawns. See Shrimp and prawns
Pudding, Tapioca, with Tequila and Strawberries, 116
Pulque, 27–29

Raspberry Meyer–Lemonade with Tequila, 70

Salad, Spinach, with Cherries, Walnuts, and Balsamic-Agave
    Vinaigrette, 93
Scallops, Seared, with Tequila-Cilantro Cream, 107
Shrimp and prawns
    Avocado Soup with Tequila-Poached Prawns and
      Caviar, 108
    Tequila-Lime Shrimp Ceviche, 88
Sopes, 91
Soups
    Avocado Soup with Tequila-Poached Prawns and
      Caviar, 108
    Corn Chowder with Roasted Tomatoes and Tequila, 89
Spinach Salad with Cherries, Walnuts, and Balsamic-Agave
    Vinaigrette, 93
Strawberries, Tapioca Pudding with Tequila and, 116

Tapioca Pudding with Tequila and Strawberries, 116
Tegroni, 81
Tejito, 68
Tequila (liquor). See also individual recipes
    aged, 31, 41
    drinking, 50–51, 54–57
    history of, 15, 23, 32–33
    latest trends in, 57–58
    mezcal vs., 30–31
    modern myths about, 30
    premium, 31, 45–46, 57–58
    production of, 31, 36–37, 40–41
    taste differences in, 58
    types of, 41, 44–45, 62–63
Tequila (town), 35–36, 49
Tomatoes
    Bloody Maria, 79
    Chipotle-Agave Glaze, 101
    Corn Chowder with Roasted Tomatoes and Tequila, 89
    Tequila-Lime Shrimp Ceviche, 88

Watermelon-Tequila Agua Fresca, 72

LIQUID / DRY MEASURE

U.S.	METRIC
$^1/_4$ teaspoon	1.25 milliliters
$^1/_2$ teaspoon	2.5 milliliters
1 teaspoon	5 milliliters
1 tablespoon	15 milliliters
1 fluid ounce	30 milliliters
$^1/_4$ cup	60 milliliters
$^1/_3$ cup	80 milliliters
$^1/_2$ cup	120 milliliters
1 pint (2 cups)	480 milliliters
1 quart	960 milliliters
1 ounce	28 grams
1 pound	454 grams
2.2 pounds	1 kilogram

OVEN TEMPERATURES

FAHRENHEIT	CELSIUS	GAS
250	120	$^1/_2$
275	140	1
300	150	2
325	160	3
350	180	4
375	190	5
400	200	6
425	220	7
450	230	8
475	240	9
500	260	10

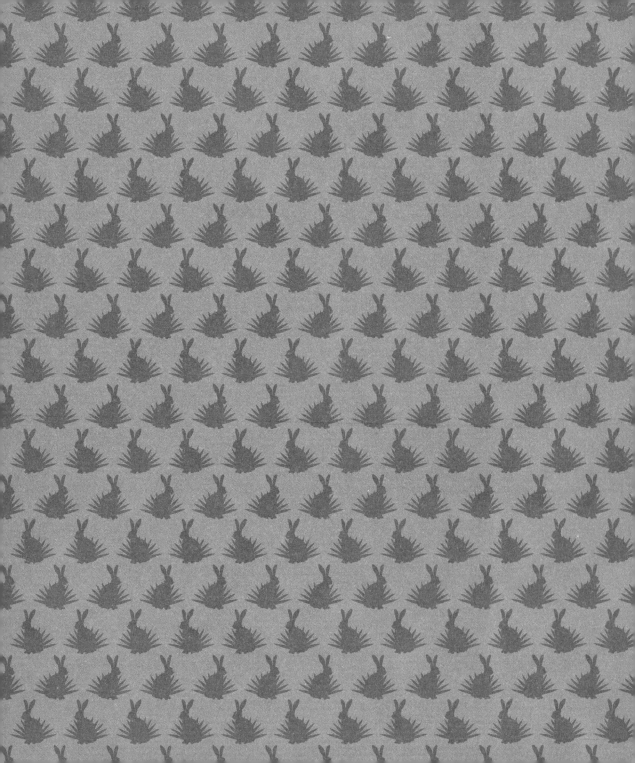